To Jim + Pat

Ever devotedly in Notre Dame.

Father Ted Hesburgh

The Terry Lectures

THE HUMANE IMPERATIVE

THE
HUMANE
IMPERATIVE

A CHALLENGE FOR THE YEAR 2000

Theodore M. Hesburgh, C.S.C.

YALE UNIVERSITY PRESS, NEW HAVEN AND LONDON

Designed by Sally Sullivan
and set in Times Roman type.
Printed in the United States of America by
Colonial Press Inc., Clinton, Mass.

Published in Great Britain, Europe, Africa, and Asia
(except Japan) by Yale University Press, Ltd., London.
Distributed in Latin America by Kaiman & Polon, Inc.,
New York City; in Australia and New Zealand by Book & Film
Services, Artarmon, N.S.W., Australia; in Japan by John
Weatherhill, Inc., Tokyo.

The Dwight Harrington Terry
Foundation Lectures
on Religion in the Light of
Science and Philosophy

The deed of gift declares that "the object of this foundation is not the promotion of scientific investigation and
discovery, but rather the assimilation and interpretation of
that which has been or shall be hereafter discovered, and
its application to human welfare, especially by the building
of the truths of science and philosophy into the structure of
a broadened and purified religion. The founder believes
that such a religion will greatly stimulate intelligent effort
for the improvement of human conditions and the ad-
vancement of the race in strength and excellence of
character. To this end it is desired that a series of lectures
be given by men eminent in their respective departments,
on ethics, the history of civilization and religion, biblical
research, all sciences and branches of knowledge which
have an important bearing on the subject, all the great laws
of nature, especially of evolution . . . also such interpreta-
tions of literature and sociology as are in accord with the
spirit of this foundation, to the end that the Christian spirit
may be nurtured in the fullest light of the world's
knowledge and that mankind may be helped to attain its
highest possible welfare and happiness upon this earth."
The present work constitutes the fortieth volume published
on this foundation.

Contents

Preface

This lectureship is a pulpit as well as a learned podium; this lecturer is above all a priest. A university founded to train men in Church and Civil State could not find a better contemporary exemplar of that ancient dual mission than Father Theodore M. Hesburgh.

In church he is a distinguished theologian. I have no qualifications to say more. In "civil state," however, I at least have a citizen's qualification to express gratitude for his energetic works.

In international reconciliation he has raised colleagues out of the ruts of self-interest—in the international control of the peaceful uses of atomic energy, and in the mobilization to help poorer nations and peoples, especially in Africa and Latin America.

Father Hesburgh's contribution to the continuing and unfinished effort to make the Declaration of Independence and the Bill of Rights a living reality for all Americans is so widely appreciated that it needs no embellishment. This ideal of equality has been kept alive, and its achievement is still a realistic hope, in considerable part because of Father Hesburgh's strenuous, stalwart championship of the cause of human dignity and equality. This reached a new and critical importance when the tide of civil rights struggle began to ebb; hope for millions would be more forlorn were it not for his steadfastness. Father Ted Hesburgh can fairly join St. Paul and affirm that "we wrestle not against flesh and blood, but against principalities, against powers, against the rulers of the darkness of this world, against spiritual wickedness in high places."

In the field of education I have some special reason to appreciate Father Ted's accomplishments, in his own university and in the leadership he has afforded the rest of us. In the harassed late sixties he combined firmness and flexibility, authority and openness, which set a standard for us all. Not widely known is his timely cable to Governor Rockefeller which persuaded the Governors' Conference of 1969 to oppose federal legislation to govern student behavior. As a result, President Nixon was persuaded not to extend the federal police power to the campuses of the nation.

Response to "student unrest," however, is not the essence of education. It is not tranquility, but dynamic progress in response to the fast pace of knowledge, and the evolving needs of a fast changing society, that stand as the true measure of Father Hesburgh's contribution through the years. He has brought the University of Notre Dame to the first rank of the nation's universities; without betraying the sponsorship of his church and his order, Father Hesburgh has achieved both the hospitality to controversy and the highest standards of rational rigor that every free university requires.

Yet because of the religious heritage of the place, most especially because of the spirituality of the man, Notre Dame is one of the few universities I know that reminds the visitor, as well as those who work and study there, that learning at heart is a morally motivated act.

This quality—spirituality—is Father Hesburgh's very special gift to those over whom he presides, those to whom he ministers, and those for whom he writes and speaks. There is no passivity in his contemplation, since the realization of God's will demands that the person throw all of himself into the cause. There is no gloom in his dedication, since it is sustained by a confidence that the Holy Spirit is at work in us all, in the world, and in the cosmos.

At a time of lowered expectations, it is good that there are voices of hope, seasoned by experience, still capable of believing that we can fashion a better world. When that belief is vindicated by history and sustained by faith, it helps to strengthen and reinvigorate us all.

KINGMAN BREWSTER, JR.

New Haven
April 1974

Prelude

What will the world be like in the year 2000? This question is the leitmotiv of all that follows. I am trying here to do the opposite of history and something short of prophecy. There is a deep conviction among modern Christians, and I count myself one of them, that we can affect the course of our times; that theological and philosophical principles can become operative in a wide variety of social, economic, political, educational, scientific, and technical activities; that as a result, the world will become better, more human, even somewhat divine and—in the incarnational sense of the English word—godly.

Because of this conviction, the modern Christian parts company with those who would relegate theology to the library and religion to the sacristy. The modern Christian refuses to place the sacred and the secular in watertight compartments well-insulated from each other. I mean this in the operational sense, not in the realm of concepts. I am not confusing the sacred and the secular as ideas or realities. But granting a conceptual separation, the modern Christian refuses to confine part of his activity to time and part to eternity. He realizes that we must travel to eternity through time, and that the light of our faith must somehow illumine and suffuse all temporal activities.* The modern Christian's prayer and action must blend and be mutually supportive. His yearnings for eternity are not unrelated to yearnings for time. He will not settle for pie in the sky. When a modern Christian speculates about the possible and probable state of the world in the year 2000, he or she is really hoping for a better condition for humanity in the days ahead, but this dream draws upon many realities and trends already at work in the world.

I should at this juncture declare myself a Christian optimist, optimistic actually because of my Christian belief—my firm faith that the Holy Spirit is at work in the world, that the great powers and forces of the religious and secular orders can find new and fruitful directions if we nudge them at the right time toward better goals.

And now is the right time. The next millennium is almost upon us, and that has only happened once before in the Christian era. The last time was a period of great foreboding. There were dire predictions of worldwide catastrophe, even of the end of the world.

* I realize that my attempts to avoid linguistic male chauvinism are clumsy—the very language reflects our inability to deal with men and women as equally important. I will use masculine pronouns to refer to all people, when I must for the sake of linguistic elegance, and continue to hope for a better solution.

As we approach the second great milestone, we actually have the capability of creating the doomsday they predicted. By our own awesome weapons we can reduce this world and everyone in it to cinders. In fact, we have enough nuclear weapons to do it several times over—and we are ever improving the technology of death and destruction.

But against this background of lurking fear I would like to speak of hope. Rather than the scenario of global catastrophe in the days ahead, I should like to project a new world that is possible and even probable if we will dare to think new thoughts, to engage in programs worthy of our hopes, and to share our vision with all who will work with us to achieve it.

The projection that follows is an essay in Christian humanism, a vision of what man and his world can be as we enter the new millennium. It is not a silly chiliastic dream; it is based on real forces now in movement, new techniques already viable, even though largely unused or used badly. And I trust I will be forgiven if I speak personally of realities with which I have been engaged here and there about the world during the past three decades.

Is the year 2000 too far ahead to be concerned about it? I think not. I may not live to usher in the second millennium, but a child born this year will only be twenty-six years old when the millennium arrives.

1 Human Progress and the Kingdom of God

I have been accused, often enough in my life, of attending to all too many secular concerns, which seem to bear no relationship to what should concern me most as a priest: God, faith, church, salvation, in a word, the Kingdom of God. The more crude objectors say, "Go back to your Bible," although I suspect I spend more time with it than any dozen of them. Others say, "You should pray more," and indeed I should—although I say with thanksgiving, not pride, that during my thirty years of priesthood I have offered Mass every day, except one, that Mass is allowed to be offered (there is no Mass on Good Friday). For me, the Mass is the greatest prayer of all, and it has carried me through many difficult days, from the South Pole to the faculty house at the University of Moscow. The Mass puts me in vital touch each day with God, and allows me to participate in His great act of redemption for everyone in the world. Whatever else I do, I am most a priest offering Mass. But these critics are still right. While I never miss my daily breviary, I should pray more. The most perceptive critics say that while human progress, justice, and peace are important, it is hardly a priority of Christians, not to mention priests, to spend most of their lives in such pursuits. As they put it, "How will you answer the saints when they ask you, 'Quid hoc ad aeternitatem'? What have all of these economic, political, cultural, educational, and other concerns to do with eternity?" A nice question. It deserves an answer, especially since I started out in a university twenty-nine years ago as a professional theologian, though I have long since ceased to consider myself one.

Before attempting, with the help of some modern theologians, to build a theological bridge between human progress and the Kingdom of God, I would like to mention briefly the basic question of transcendence that must never be forgotten in discussion of this kind. The German theologian Joseph Ratzinger has said that the two most important issues in theology today are *politics* (questions, for example, of neo-Marxism, violence, the true meaning of liberation) and *spirituality* (for instance, the content of our hope, in what way God is the basis of our life). The issue of spirituality is the transcendent one, although the two issues are closely related. As Ratzinger puts it,

> For me, priority must be given to the urgent question of how to discover God in our life. . . .

I'm talking about what may awkwardly be described as coming into contact with God, finding Him as the basis of our being and all of our acts—discovering that real sense of interiority which gives us both an independence from the things of this world and a new relationship to them.

In prayer and meditation we can find the tranquility and the transforming power of the presence of God. Union with God is, ultimately, the only basis on which our community with others can rest. Our interior liberty enables us to live in community, and to see and serve the needs of all, especially the poor. The type of committed detachment which is the by-product of this interior liberty destroys the roots of all forms of exploitation, including the lust for power inherent in political activity; and it opens the eyes to the injustices that are concealed in every system.*

This primacy of the spiritual and of spirituality in one's personal life will save theologians from becoming either academic pedants, speaking only to each other on esoteric subjects, or aliens in the land of faith they should primarily, though not exclusively, inhabit. Transcendence does not mean unconcern, but ultimately greater concern, freely given, without compromise. Living theology makes all of this possible and in fact necessary for the theologian.

* Cited in Desmond O'Grady, "Lost in the Shouting: The Meaning of Vatican II," U.S. Catholic 38, no. 10 (October, 1973): 34.

Theology strives to be the orderly spiritual expression of Christian wisdom, as it was so well during the ages of the Greek and Latin Fathers of the Church. It became in the Middle Ages, under the genius of theologians like Abelard and Albert and Aquinas, a strict intellectual discipline wherein faith and reason met, discussed, and illuminated each other—as was so well said: *Fides quaerens intellectum et intellectus quaerens fidem.* Faith seeking understanding and understanding seeking faith. As the sciences have developed in recent centuries, there has been mutual advantage in theology, the science of faith, meeting and discussing with the secular sciences all of the insights they each bring to man's total understanding of himself, his world, and his God. All human knowledge can benefit from theological reflection, and theology should concern itself with the implications of new scientific understanding for the world of faith. But all too little of this intellectual linkage takes place in this world of isolation and specialization.

Today theology must be increasingly involved in a critical reflection on the problems of the world and modern man's place in the world as he works out his salvation and seeks the Kingdom of God. As Yves Congar said, "If the Church wishes to deal with the real questions of the modern world and to attempt to respond to them . . . it must open, as it were, a new chapter of theologico-pastoral epistemology. Instead of using only revelation and tradition as starting points, as classical theology has generally done, it must start with facts and questions derived from the world and from history." * This new theological attitude has led to the introduction of the word *orthopraxis,* referring to critical theological reflection, and especially action regarding a Christian's life and commitment in a very complex world, according to the light of the gospel message. *Orthopraxis* is used in contrast to *orthodoxy,* which concerns doctrine, generally in the abstract order of ideas. The Dutch theologian Edward Schillebeeckx puts it bluntly, though a bit too antagonistically and absolutely for me: "It is evident that thought is necessary for action. But the Church for centuries devoted her attention to formulating truths and, meanwhile, did almost nothing to better the world. In other words, the Church focused on orthodoxy and left orthopraxis in the hands of nonmembers and nonbelievers." And later, "The hermeneutics of the Kingdom of God consists especially in making the world a better place. Only in this way will I be able to discover what the Kingdom of God means." † Such statements are most nuanced in context, but their import for our purpose is clear enough.

Granted that modern theology can and should be deeply involved in the complex problems of modern man and his world—which in turn need the illumination of the faith and the inspiration of Christian wisdom as never before—that still leaves unresolved

* *Situations et taches* (Paris: Les Editions du Cerf, 1967), p. 72.
† "La Teologia," *Los Catolicos Holandeses* (Bilbao: Desclee de Brouwer, 1970), p. 29.

the involvement of the Christian. How does all of this "secular" activity relate to the mission of the Church, the life of the Christian, salvation, and the Kingdom of God?

There is an integral, organic unity to the life of a Christian. In the broadest sense, the committed Christian is, like Christ the Savior, engaged in the creation of a new world and a new man. As Vatican II put it, "We are witnesses to the birth of a new humanism, one in which man is defined first by his responsibility towards his brothers and towards history." One could add, and toward history in the making, the new creation, for this same constitution begins by saying that the Church today must share "the joys and the hopes, the griefs and the anxieties, of men of this age." * The presumption spelled out later in the Constitution on "The Church in the Modern World" is that we are going to do something about these hopes and anxieties, that we are going to be engaged in some new creative and salvific action as Christians.

Creation and salvation are deeply allied in the Old Testament and the New. A modern theologian, the Peruvian Gustavo Gutierrez, uses this linkage to establish a connection between Christian social praxis, working for the new creation, and salvation.

When we assert that man fulfills himself by continuing the work of creation by the means of

* *Gaudium et Spes*, in *The Documents of Vatican II* (Guild Press, 1966), p. 261; p. 199.

his labor, we are saying that he places himself, by this very fact, within an all-embracing salvific process. To work, to transform this world, is to become a man and to build the human community; it is to save. Likewise, to struggle against misery and exploitation and to build a just society is already to be a part of the saving action, which is moving towards its complete fulfillment. All this means that building the temporal city is not simply a stage of "humanization" or "pre-evangelization" as was held in theology up until a few years ago. Rather it is to become part of a saving process which embraces the whole of man and all human history. Any theological reflection on human work and social praxis ought to be rooted in this fundamental affirmation. . . .

The conclusion to be drawn . . . is clear: salvation embraces all men and the whole man; the liberating action of Christ—the Word made man in this history and not in a history marginal to the real life of man—is at the heart of the historical current of humanity; the struggle for a just society is in its own right very much a part of salvation history.*

One can say this without identifying all temporal progress with the building of the Kingdom of God, which is by nature eternal. However, while there is a distinction between temporal progress and the

* *Theology of Liberation* (Maryknoll, New York: Orbis Books, 1973), p. 160; p. 168.

growth of the Kingdom, they are and should be closely related in the minds and motives of Christians working for peace and justice; indeed, they must be part of the total endeavor of the one life we live.

There is, then, a profound unity in the divine plan for man, creation, salvation, and the Kingdom of God. Redemption embraces the totality of creation, and those working for a new man and a new earth are very much creating, and redeeming the times as well. There is one history of mankind. It is not static but dynamic, and all that we say, propose, dream, and hope for the development of mankind in our day should be seen in the broadest possible historical context, which is also eschatological. Looking ahead to that ultimate Kingdom of Justice, Peace, and Love validates as nothing else can for the Christian his or her efforts to seek eternity through time, to love God by loving men, to serve and to create, to build a community of men that may also, by God's grace, be a Kingdom of God. Anything less is unworthy of a Christian.

Believing all of this profoundly, and relying on the words the good Lord proposes to use in judging us all, "What you did to one of these, my least brethren, you did it to me," I find no dissonance in a Christian's involvement in the world. In fact, I would be deeply disturbed about a Christian, a Christian community, or a church that did not concern itself seriously in all these temporal matters. As we read in

Isaiah, "Your countless sacrifices, what are they to me, says the Lord. I am sated with the whole offerings of rams. . . . the offer of your gifts is useless, the reek of sacrifices is abhorrent to me. . . . though you offer countless prayers, I will not listen. There is blood on your hands. . . . cease to do evil and learn to do right, pursue justice and champion the oppressed; give the orphan his rights, plead the widow's cause." (Isa. 1:10–17)

The good Lord left no doubt that He identified the love of neighbor with the love of God Himself. When we feed the hungry, give drink to the thirsty, clothe the naked, or visit the imprisoned, we do it to Him. When we refuse, we refuse Him. We then love neither God nor neighbor.

I would like to conclude this *apologia pro vita mea* by quoting a passage written for those who spend their lives among the poor and suffering in the missions of Latin America:

All the dynamism of the cosmos, and of human history, the movement towards the creation of a more just and fraternal world, the overcoming of social inequities among men, the efforts, so urgently needed on our continent, to liberate man from all that depersonalizes him—physical and moral misery, ignorance and hunger, as well as the awareness of human dignity, all these originate, are transformed, and reach their perfection in the saving work of Christ. In Him and through Him, salvation is present at the heart of man's history.*

May we all be a part of this evolving history, this creative and salvific act.

* "La Pastoral en las Missiones de America Latinas," cited in Gustavo Gutierrez, *Theology of Liberation*, p. 178.

2 The Power of Ecumenism

Of all the opportunities bearing upon the shape of the world in the year 2000, and beyond in the new millennium, clearly the most important movements afoot today are those that concern the unity of mankind. One of the strongest of these is ecumenism, not only in the Christian, but in the larger world-religion dimension. I speak here of a professedly theological reality, but its profound influence is not only transreligious but transcultural, transnational, deeply human and universal. And it bears directly on a new and growing unity among more than two thirds of mankind.

My most serious introduction to ecumenism came in April of 1964, the third year of Vatican Council II, when Pope Paul VI asked me to visit him in Rome to discuss a special project. One of the greatest experiences he had derived from the council was the opportunity of meeting the many theologians who were observers on behalf of the Protestant, Anglican, and Orthodox churches, he explained. He had found them wonderful men, dedicated to theology, deep in their faith, holy in their lives, and like himself, yearning for the unity of all Christians in our times.

The Holy Father had also been deeply impressed by two remarkable experiences in the preceding months. That January he had met and embraced Athenagoras, the Patriarch of Constantinople, now Istanbul. After more than a thousand years of painful separation—beginning at the time of the first millennium, when the western and eastern, the Latin and Greek branches of Christianity were separated by schism—the heads of these two ancient churches for the first time encountered each other, in the only place on earth where this was possible, where it all began: Jerusalem, the holy city, the city of peace.

The second experience was the Holy Father's meeting with all the non-Catholic observers. The speaker for the observers was Kristen Skydsgaard of Copenhagen. He reflected a thought inspired by another observer, Oscar Cullmann of Basel, that the Holy Father should capture the magic of the hour by creating a place where the Christian theological fraternity born during the council might be continued—an institute where the mystery of salvation, which we all share and cherish, might be studied together in an atmosphere of brotherhood and prayer. The Holy Father asked whether, as president of the International Federation of Catholic Universities, I might not be able to establish such an institute—in Jerusalem.

The following day, the council members of the

federation agreed, and established a provisional commission. Then on Thanksgiving weekend, 1965, an international group of university theologians from all the Christian churches agreed to form an academic council to try to realize the project, which from that day was under their direction. Subsequently, the International Federation of Catholic Universities bowed out, delegating to the University of Notre Dame the multitudinous financial, architectural, and administrative responsibilities of the project, now under the policy direction of the Academic Council of ecumenical theologians.

Everything conspired against the project. The Six Day War and the ensuing turmoil caused financial problems, with widespread incredulity at the thought of building a $2 million institute in Jerusalem, of all places, especially at this time. But land was obtained; a generous donor, the late I. A. O'Shaughnessy, shared the vision and donated the cost of the building; and it did get built. It is reputed to be the most beautiful Christian building in Jerusalem, seeming to grow out of its olive and pine clad hilltop of Tantur, between Jerusalem and Bethlehem. It has been operating these past three years, with those who first dreamed it occasionally in attendance, including Skydsgaard and Cullmann.

This story illustrates two realities we all need to recognize. First, the impossible is possible with faith and hope and especially love. And second, Protestants, Orthodox, and Catholics can move together toward unity if they pray and live together as they theologize. As the one who probably worried most as all of this moved along, I was immensely edified by my brothers who shared the dream, who worked side by side to make it come true, who never lost faith or hope, and were prodigal in their love. All of this happened against the background of one thousand years of misunderstandings between Orthodox and Latin Christians, four and a half centuries of bitter and unchristian strife between Catholics and Protestants. But we do share our faith in Christ, our Savior, and it brought us through every crisis and difficulty. In the place that has been called the umbilical of the world, a place sacred to Moslems, Jews, and Christians, we are living, praying, and working together.

This experience left me with the profound conviction that the third of humanity that calls itself Christian need no longer be divided by past errors, for which we are all guilty. We are determined to be one again as the good Lord desires. As the Holy Father remarked in that first conversation about the project, many of the religious diversities that have developed during so many centuries of disunion may be looked upon as rich developments of the Holy Spirit within the total Christian community. Unity does not mean uniformity. Nothing good that has developed to enrich faith and prayer and community life need be lost as long as we now grow together in the unity of our faith, hope, and love.

Will the next millennium see Christian unity emerge from centuries of division and strife? I believe it will, and further perceive that the faithful are far

ahead of all the clerical bureaucracies in learning to
live together in Christian love and understanding.
This new Christian peace dawning under the powerful inspiration of the Holy Spirit has enormous
potential for the unity of mankind in our day, for
there are fewer bonds more cohesive than bonds born
of religious faith. It once held the Western world
together against almost insupportable strains. In the
new millennium it may bring together an even wider
world of religions, in the broader ecumenism now
burgeoning between Christians and non-Christians.

Too long have we taken for granted that "East is
East and West is West and never the twain shall
meet." Young people today are much more interested
in what unites humankind than in what has so long
divided it. The non-Christian religions have more
than a billion members. One thinks first of religions
of the Book, those closest to Christianity—Islam and
Judaism, religions of the sons of Abraham. Then
there are the Hindus, Buddhists, Confucians, Shintos,
animists, and many others, mostly Eastern and
African. For centuries all of these religions and their
followers were for most Christians simply "others,"
or worse, heathens or pagans. We never stopped to
consider the strong bridges of essentially religious
belief that link us together and could contribute
mightily to the essential unity of mankind and to
peace among us in our separated worlds.

Take, for example, the four following beliefs,
shared essentially by all the great religions (with the

possible exception of Buddhism regarding a personal creator god):

1. *Belief in God:* conceived and named variously, but nonetheless a pervasive key reality transcending all other reality and somehow explaining all other reality. A God who somehow made us, somehow ineffably speaks to us and hears our prayers, a God found in so many ways that not to believe in Him has always been a minority position among humans.

2. *Belief in a moral order of good and evil:* somehow created by God and somehow supervised by Him. A godlike man is a good man, and an evil man is ungodly. Whatever the divergences in moral belief across religions and cultures, the great broad lines of what the medievals called the natural law or the law of peoples—*lex gentium*—is generally, at the basic level of doing good and avoiding evil, taken to be binding on every man, woman, and child of whatever time, place, or condition. We are understood to know the broad lines of good and evil by an inner voice called conscience, often conceived to be the voice of God speaking within us and to us.

3. *The primacy of the spiritual over the material:* this belief, like the previous one, has closely linked religion to culture. Man is special in that he evaluates in a spiritual sense, creates in his life and works an inner beauty that transcends money, power, and prestige. The great spiritual values—love, justice, honesty, compassion, courage, fidelity, and so many others—are what enrich a person's character and life

and works. The spiritual, not the material, is the factor most important in fulfilling a person and making him or her happy.

4. *Immortality:* in whatever form, is among the deepest yearnings of all religious beliefs. Ultimate death would be ultimate negation of everything precious to men and women: consciousness, self-hood, loving relationships with family and friends, justice and mercy at work, reward for good and punishment for the evil, an end to pain and the misery of separation, and, ultimately, that great burning hope of eternal union with God. Life is fundamentally tenacious, and religion makes eternal life a most tenacious hope. I have placed this belief last because, while it is in many ways the most universal bridge of all among religions, it takes so many forms that it is the most difficult to enunciate or define. But it is there and it perdures. Even in our Christian religion, it is left the most vague of all revelations. The good Lord said only, as if to tease us, "Eye has not seen, and ear has not heard, and it has not entered into the mind of man to imagine what God has prepared for those who love Him." And our creed concludes simply, "I believe . . . in eternal life. Amen."

Man, so often divided in so many ways over so many millennia, ought to recognize these strong bonds that can ultimately unite him to others on this planet. One way to begin is to take these four beliefs, and others that suggest themselves, and see what enlightenment we receive in discussing them with theologians of the other great world religions. This is starting to happen at our Christian Ecumenical Institute at Tantur. The important point is that mankind believing has been separated by its religious beliefs, and the very opposite should be true in the next millennium. I believe that the new and growing interest in world religions, evidenced by the fact that even my church now has a Secretariat for Christian Unity, a Secretariat for Non-Christian Religions, and a Secretariat for Nonbelievers, indicates that the new millennium will see a union of mankind in a growing active ecumenism, in both the Christian and world-religion dimensions.

Let me illustrate what we have been missing with a passage from the Hindu poet, Rabindranath Tagore:

Leave this chanting and singing and telling of beads! Whom dost thou worship in this lonely dark corner of a temple with doors all shut? Open thine eyes and see thy God is not before thee!

He is there where the tiller is tilling the hard ground and where the pathmaker is breaking stones. He is with them in sun and in shower, and his garment is covered with dust. Put off thy holy mantle and even like him come down on the dusty soil!

Deliverance? Where is this deliverance to be found? Our master himself has joyfully taken upon him the bonds of creation; he is bound with us all forever.

Come out of thy meditations and leave aside thy

flowers and incense! What harm is there if thy
clothes become tattered and stained? Meet him
and stand by him in toil and in sweat of thy brow.*

What Christian could not recite these lines in prayer
and come closer to God? Yet most Christians would
never suspect that an eastern Hindu could write of
God so incarnationally as this.

It might also be worthy of note that one of the best
known Christian monks, Thomas Merton, Brother
Louis of the silent Trappists, died in Bangkok while
discussing monasticism with his Buddhist counter-
parts. He said, "We have to begin to understand
Eastern religions so that we, in turn, might rediscover
our Christianity." And that other great visionary of
the unity of mankind, Teilhard de Chardin, died on
Easter Sunday—the day of the Resurrection—as he
had hoped he might, because that day symbolizes the
ultimate convergence of man and God. Many paths
lead toward the ultimate, the omega of human
progress meeting the pleroma of Christian hope,
nature and grace meeting and embracing eternally.
Two small coincidences perhaps, but they indicate to
me a force at work that should see great fruition in
the next millennium. Maranatha. Come Lord Jesus.

* Amiya Chakravarty, trans., *A Tagore Reader* (New York: Macmillan
Co., 1961), p. 295.

3   Human Dignity and Civil Rights

The second great trend that can and should profoundly affect the condition of humankind in the
next millennium is the growing consciousness of
human dignity, human rights, and human development. These are concepts with profound philosophical and theological underpinnings, but the realization
and acceptance of their importance, especially for
women, children, the poor, and racial and religious
minorities, has been a long time coming. In many
ways, a consciousness of human dignity and a respect
for human rights has spurred man's march toward
civilization and culture. As in all other human
developments, there have been peaks and valleys; in
this one, more valleys than peaks until very recently.

I think it a fair statement that in man's long history
men and women have been mainly slave and seldom
free. In those millennia of unwritten history that we
are trying to reconstruct archeologically and anthro-
pologically, searching in the deep darkness for a few
identifiable objects, we discern one abiding fact:

early man had a short painful life, most of which was spent in the all-consuming effort to stay alive, and an early death. There was little nicety, little culture, little humanity, little beauty. As Gliddings of Brown University found in his digs at the Onion Portage of the Kobuk River above the Arctic Circle in Northern Alaska, each of thirty layers of human artifacts, stretching back some eight thousand years, told a similar story. There were some remains of a primitive shelter against the cold, some fish and caribou bones, some campfire remnants, and some human bones sprinkled with red ochre in the hope of a better world beyond. Food, shelter, and hope beyond. Perhaps a less grim story in less harsh climes, but generally the same outline: to maintain life, not really to live in any deeply human sense. Man was a slave to cold and heat, hunger and illness, fear, superstition, and igno-rance. But he kept yearning and moving upward. When the ideograph, the symbol, and the alphabet begin to record human history, man's existence emerges as a bit more human, with the trappings of culture and urbanization seen here and there around the world, but slavery still very much a reality for the majority of humankind. The earlier forms of slavery give way to political and economic slavery—more sophisticated, but slavery all the same—the basic denial of human dignity, rights, and equality.

At the beginning of the Christian era, St. Paul wrote a letter to a slave owner, Philemon, asking him not to free, but to deal kindly with Onesimus, a runaway slave who had been good to Paul and whom

Paul was returning to him. Despite the new human vista of Christianity, official slavery coexisted with it four hundred years after the death of Christ. When it reoccurred a millennium later, Christians were the best customers of the Arab traders. One should visit the island of Gorée, in the harbor of Dakar, to sense what it must have meant to cram 450 slaves into a small prison to await the next slave ship. It adds to the horror to recall that some 20 million slaves died on their trip across the Atlantic. Throughout the world, human dignity and human rights continued to exist in travesty rather than reality because of these and other human and natural forces.

Western civilization occasionally reached for peaks like the Magna Carta. Centuries later, there were great statements like *"liberté, égalité, fraternité,"* of the French Revolution, or those great documents that ushered in the birth of our country nearly two hundred years ago. But even then the majority of the first Americans could not exercise the fundamental political right of voting, because they were slaves, women, not property owners, or too young. We have since redressed these injustices, but at the initially ineffective price of a civil war in the case of slaves, and in the last decade's revolution in the case of the young. Even now, women are awaiting the ratification of an amendment to assure their constitutional rights.

The most amazing aspect of the growing consciousness of human dignity is how recently it even began to blossom. Not until twenty-five years ago,

after millennia of slow upward strivings, was a
Universal Declaration of Human Rights set down at
all. But when I attended, as head of the Vatican
delegation, the twentieth anniversary celebration of
the United Nations' Universal Declaration held in
Teheran, Iran, two sad realities impressed me. First,
practically none of the large nations had yet ratified
the two protocols—one on civil and political rights,
the other on economic, social, educational, and
cultural rights—that flowed from the Universal Declaration, and none of the smaller nations was really
observing these rights either. Second, the first week of
the conference was mainly given over to fighting
between Arabs and Israeli, Indians and Pakistani,
Northern and Southern Africans, and others too
numerous to mention. My own contribution, I fear,
was to scold them for acting like this:

> . . . The understandable frustration is most evi-
> dent in the way that so many delegates find it
> easier to accuse others of their shortcomings than
> to look deeply into their own consciences, individ-
> ual and national. What would be the effect of this
> conference, if instead of pointing our fingers or
> aiming our invectives at one another, we looked
> honestly and sincerely at ourselves, to measure,
> each his own country, against the great ideals
> enunciated in the Universal Declaration on
> Human Rights?
>
> Our delegation is especially intrigued by the
> imaginative Costa Rican suggestion of a high

commissioner for human rights who might become a worldwide ombudsman, especially if the post could be filled by someone recognized everywhere for personal integrity and high moral leadership. He or she could be helped by a committee chosen for high competence, with adequate national and regional support, governmental and nongovernmental, and with ultimate juridical support from national, regional, and international courts. The commissioner could indeed become the living focus for the problem that so concerns us here in this conference. The problem of human rights is so universal that it transcends all other problems that face humanity and the United Nations. It is obvious to our delegation, as to all of you, that this conference will not reach a successful conclusion if we do not agree on some realistic mechanisms to translate words into deeds, ideals into reality, hopes into achievement. The strong agreement of this conference on the necessity of a high commissioner for human rights would be a minimal first step in this direction.

One cannot speak of hopes without underlining the fact that the younger generation, half of the world's population today, is conscious of the much we have said and the little we have done about their deep concern for the world that we have created, with all its inequities, with its racism, with its perduring prejudices, with its continuing and flagrant discrimination. I speak as one who has spent all of his adult life in a university, with young

people. Our younger generation will not wait
forever for peaceful solutions to this burning
problem of human equality. The young have only
one life to live here on earth and it is now before
them, filled with a whole series of tantalizing
opportunities. They know that the human situation
need not be what it is, as we permit it to be. If we
do not act now, and act together, and act effectively, this conference will be in fact a sad celebration of a very happy and promising moment
twenty years ago. The younger generation is being
constantly and strongly tempted to violence, violence that solves nothing and deepens human
misery, even the misery of the young. But if we do
not act effectively, what other alternative do we
leave them?

Love or hatred, peace or violence, order or
disorder: these are the real choices that face
humanity, young and old, and this conference
today. Strange as it may seem to us, our continuing
apathy in the face of worldwide and inhuman
injustice makes the young of this world even doubt
the meaning of the words we use in expressing
humanity's ideal, makes them even more doubt our
sincerity and our courage.

Despite all this, the Universal Declaration of
Human Rights does exist and it does represent the
most complete statement of its kind in the history of
humanity. Our present problem is to make it less an
ideal and more a reality, to persuade all the nations

of the world to ratify the two protocols, to see that their provisions are observed throughout the world: in realizing the inherent God-given dignity of every person; in achieving freedom to be truly human; in creating a new equality of opportunity to make the world more humane and more just.

One would hope that for many reasons, but mainly because of our great traditions and growing consciousness of human dignity and equality, the United States might take a leading role in this endeavor. Nothing else—neither power, nor might, nor wealth, nor prestige—would speak more persuasively to the rest of mankind. In so many ways, the United States is the microcosm of the total problem everywhere. We have every race in our population. Color is more often a cause of prejudice than race, and again we have more colored citizens than any majority white nation on earth—more blacks than the total white population of Canada, more browns than all the whites in Australia. While we are largely a Christian nation, we have more Jews, by three times, than Israel, and we have every variety of Christian under the sun. We are an amalgam of every European nationality, culture, and language, and in exchange students alone we have thousands of Africans, Asians, and Latin Americans. It is as if the good Lord set us up as a laboratory experiment to pioneer the observance of human rights, dignity, and equality in a most pluralistic world.

Despite our obvious failings, and they are many, I believe that in the decade of the sixties we made more

progress in solving what Gunnar Myrdal called "the
American dilemma" than ever before in our history.
Moreover, no other nation, ancient or modern, has
made similar advances in so short a period of time. I
think that today we need the encouragement of this
fact to keep trying and not to lose hope, despite
temporary setbacks.

When the United States Commission on Civil
Rights was established by the Congress in 1957 to
ascertain the condition of civil rights in America and
to advise the president and Congress regarding
corrective action, we found the situation bad indeed.
The law creating the commission was the first attempt in over eighty years to legislate federally for
civil rights. And we of the commission were generally
considered a fairly impotent body: six members
representing both political parties, three Northerners
and three Southerners, five whites and one black—
armed only with the power to subpoena persons and
documents and to publicize our findings and our
corrective advice to the president and Congress. It
seems almost miraculous that over the next fifteen
years about 75 percent of our suggestions were
enacted into federal law, even though they were often
dismissed as ridiculous by one President, only to be
endorsed by the next.

At the commission's beginning a decade and a half
ago, several million black Americans in the southern
states could not even register to vote; black children
by law had to attend inferior black primary and
secondary schools; black students were not welcome

at Southern state universities and their numbers were minuscule at white private and public colleges and universities across the country. As a result, there were very few black professionals—four black lawyers out of over two thousand lawyers in Mississippi, for example, where no white lawyer would touch a civil rights case. One of the black lawyers wouldn't either. Black Americans throughout the South faced dozens of daily indignities. They could not eat in most restaurants, rent rooms in most hotels, drink at most fountains and bars, sit where they pleased in buses, trains, theaters—even churches—could not even be buried in cemeteries with whites. They could, however, pay taxes, die for their country in a war, and do most of the menial work, North and South. What was a *de jure* indignity in the South was often enough a *de facto* indignity in the North, because of federally financed and sustained housing patterns.

We should remember this tragic human situation, even though much of it has now passed into history. We should remember Rosa Parks, who refused, at long last, to move to the back of the bus when her feet were tired after a long day's work—thus starting the Montgomery bus boycott and a whole sequence of sit-ins, eat-ins, drink-ins, pray-ins, sleep-ins, and, in fact, the whole revolution of the sixties for the achievement of human dignity and human rights. We should remember Martin Luther King and Medgar Evers and all who suffered and died to make the country awake to its plight. We should remember President Lyndon Johnson, who stood before a joint session of Congress and declared from his heart, "We shall overcome," as we did with the passage of the great omnibus Civil Rights Act of 1964, the Voting Act of 1965, and the Housing Act of 1968.

Some have said that the law does not really change anything, but in these cases it did. Public accommodations were opened to blacks overnight. While only 3 percent of the southern school districts were desegregated in the decade following the Supreme Court's *Brown* decision of 1954, over 70 percent of the districts were desegregated in the five years following the enactment of Title VI of the 1964 act. There were only about six elected black officials in the South when blacks there largely could not vote. More than a thousand were elected in 1972. Blacks are seen more frequently now in business and the professions, in all the great universities of the land, slowly but surely on their faculties, on corporate boards, as mayors of great cities like Cleveland, Newark, Atlanta, Detroit, and Los Angeles. And as the world did not end with this sudden change—it was enriched and improved—the law did prove educational.

I have spoken mainly of the rights of blacks and the sudden breakthrough they made in the sixties. To be honest, I should add that about twelve million Spanish-speaking Americans and about a million Indians still await their breakthrough. Orientals still have special problems, too. Women are better than half our population and I need not remind you of the new stirrings of women's liberation here in America and all around the world. And because I have been on the side of all who could not speak effectively for themselves, I must also speak for those who have no voice at all, the unborn children who are so cavalierly deprived of the most basic right of all, the right to life, without which all other human rights are meaningless. Each of us once was what these unborn children, of whatever stage of development, now are. No one of us would like to have been deprived of the days and years of human life we have enjoyed. Millions of unborn children are now, within the law—the law of man, not of God—being so denied. I must speak for them and their most basic right to live. And I do. I hope that more of them will survive to enjoy the new millennium and to contribute to a new dignity for all mankind, once their own has been recognized and they have been allowed to live and love as all of us have. Later, I will speak of the children of the underdeveloped world, half of whom die before the age of six.

In general, I believe we must broaden our view of the range of human rights that should be guaranteed to our people and protected by our laws. The rights of individuals in this country have been largely a collection of political and civil liberties rooted in a centuries-old tradition. More is required than political and civil rights to secure the dignity of human beings. We must move beyond political and civil rights and afford protection to economic and social rights as well. Too often we deal with social and economic issues in this country as problems, as the discharge of minimal responsibilities to take care of the needy. When we have acted to provide economic or social benefits we have viewed such actions as bestowing a privilege. Our people have political and civil rights; in economic, social and cultural areas, we dispense privileges. This is too narrow a view.

Its narrowness was made clear to me at the Teheran conference mentioned above, where I observed the split between the definition of rights in the Western world and in the socialist world. To socialist governments, concern for human rights focuses essentially on social and economic rights. We, on the other hand, have focused more on political and civil rights. The chairman of the United States delegation to the Teheran conference was Roy Wilkins, who, in a brilliant speech, attempted to bridge the differences. He observed that "the authors of the Four Freedoms did not engage in the sterile and useless debate over the relative merits and priorities of civil and political as compared with economic and social rights. They knew that all these freedoms were interdependent." He spoke of the necessity to make an amalgam of civil, political, social, and economic rights—a goal toward which we should all dedicate ourselves.

But to return to my original thought, will America give leadership to the world in the area of human dignity, rights, and equality of opportunity, because of the special tradition of our country and our special situation as a nation of many religions, races, nationalities, cultures, and colors? Or will we default, just as the world is beginning to awake to the burning need for the recognition of human dignity and rights everywhere? We gave great and unique leadership to all the world in the sixties. What has begun to go wrong in the seventies?

First, Americans are impatient. We like quick victories, facile solutions, and are soon bored by lingering problems. That is why our typical art form, the western movie, always ends by quickly killing off all the opposition, the bad guys. There is no more lingering problem among all mankind than prejudice. While laws can correct inequitable situations and educate while doing this, prejudice must be faced and conquered every hour of every day by every individual within his inner self. No law, not even God's, can effect understanding, tolerance, magnanimity within us. This is a challenge that each of us faces, each day. No quick victory here.

Second, the problem of civil rights in the sixties was easier for northerners because it primarily affected the South. Everyone is good at practicing virtue at a distance. When the problem began to move north, with a total approach to open housing, desegregation of schools by busing, greater equality of opportunity in employment in the northern cities and their suburbs, then the northern liberals began to act as defensively as the southern conservatives had. Not *my* neighborhood, not *my* child's school, not *my* university, not *my* club, not *my* job. As the old farmer said, "It depends on whose kid has the measles."

Third, the fast pace of progress in the sixties was slowed in the seventies because politicians, like

sharks smelling blood, began to see political profit in
catering to the deeply implanted prejudices and fears
of Americans who perhaps felt that there had been
too much progress too quickly or, more honestly, that
they were personally threatened by the onward
march of progress. New banners of ethnicity were
waved; idealism was replaced by political pragma-
tism; leaders followed instead of leading; the slow-
down and the slipback began, led by the most
powerful officials in the land.

The same burning question remains: Are we going
to stand still on basic human rights, slip back, or
move forward? We have come down from a high
peak in our history and are presently in a valley. The
rest of the world is hardly heroic in this matter
either—witness the slaughter of the Hutus in Ru-
anda, the plight of the Bihari in Bangladesh, the
fratricidal hatreds of the sons of Abraham, Arabs
and Israeli, in the Middle East, and the continuing
vendetta between North and South Vietnamese and
Koreans. Yet with all the burden of ingrained
prejudice and hatred, I believe that our age, more
than any previous one, knows that this is wrong, that
it is suicidal on so small a planet as ours. We do have
our Universal Declaration of Human Rights, which is
light years beyond the statements of the Magna Carta
and the French and American revolutionary documents, although its rhetoric has yet to yield deeds in
many areas of the world. I believe we must keep our
eyes on that peak. And I deeply believe that given the
proper kind of courageous and inspirational leader-

ship from the officials of church and state on all levels, America will continue the upward march into the next millennium. We have our 200th birthday as an added incentive to make the promises of our Constitution and Bill of Rights come true. More than the military shield of America, the world will need, today and in the millennium to come, the example of its conscientious care for the manifold assemblage of citizens that makes this country unique in the world, *e pluribus unum.* Might the whole world be thus in the next millennium.

4   Population and the Green Revolution

I remarked as I began that the modern Christian
believes he can make his theological and philosophical principles operative in the affairs and problems of
his times. The following is an exercise in that belief.
And I promised that my projections for the next
millennium would be hopeful and optimistic, so you
may expect a bright rather than a dismal preview,
although I concede that the worst could happen. But
however one projects his or her hopes for the next
millennium, central to every consideration will be the
human person. It is the person who shares the hope
and sees it realized or denied in his or her life. It is
the person who has faith and who loves his brothers
and sisters in truth and justice. It is the person who
enjoys or is denied his or her rights. It is the person
who is at the heart of all earthly history, who is
hungry and thirsty, who seeks shelter and warmth;
who is born, suffers, enjoys, works, gives life and
love; who persecutes, hates, or is violent; who makes

war or peace, builds or destroys, dies; it is the person who makes these choices.

One finds surprisingly little today, even in philosophy, on the human person. The best description that I have found comes from another Terry lecturer, Jacques Maritain.

What do we mean precisely when we speak of the human person? When we say that a man is a person, we do not mean merely that he is an individual, in the sense that an atom, a blade of grass, a fly or an elephant is an individual. Man is an individual who holds himself in hand by intelligence and will. He does not exist only in a physical manner. He has a spiritual superexistence through knowledge and love; he is, in a way, a universe in himself, a microcosm, in which the great universe in its entirety can be encompassed through knowledge; and through love, he can give himself completely to beings who are to him, as it were, other selves, a relation for which no equivalent can be found in the physical world. The human person possesses these characteristics because in the last analysis man, this flesh and these perishable bones which are animated and activated by a divine fire, exists "from the womb to the grave" by virtue of the very existence of his soul, which dominates time and death. Spirit is the root of personality. The notion of personality thus involves that of totality and independence; no matter how poor and crushed he may be, a person, as such, is a whole and subsists in an independent manner. To say that man is a person is to say that in the depths of his being he is more a whole than a part, and more independent than servile. It is to say that he is a minute fragment of matter that is at the same time a universe, a beggar who communicates with absolute being, mortal flesh whose value is eternal, a bit of straw into which heaven enters. It is this metaphysical mystery that religious thought points to when it says that the person is the image of God. The value of the person, his dignity and his rights belong to the order of things naturally sacred which bear the imprint of the Father of being, and which have in Him the end of their movement.*

Since the person is so central, it seems appropriate to say a few words about population. Obviously, everything said of persons will be conditioned by the number of people involved.

I do not believe that anyone or any group—not even the Club of Rome with their computers—has absolute wisdom about the precise number of people that would make an ideal population for our earth. Certain truths about the numbers are, however, absolute. A planet with finite, life-sustaining resources, some of which are being completely exhausted (oil, for example) cannot endure a constant geometric growth in population without courting global disaster. And the net population growth in the

* *Principes d'une politique humaniste* (Paris: Paul Hartmann, 1945), pp. 15-16.

decade of the sixties, 700 million, equaled the total net growth of the nineteenth century. If the present rate of growth were to continue until 2074, a century hence, we would be adding a billion persons a year, the present world's population every three and a half years.

Obviously, that is not going to happen. The sad fact is that we are doing an inadequate job of feeding, housing, educating, and caring for the health of our present population. I believe we must both slow down our present net world population growth of 1.3 million persons a week and vastly improve our care for those already dwelling on earth, so as to achieve progress on our present problems without further complicating them while we are trying to solve them.

Numbers are very much a part of the problem of development at present because the greatest population growth is taking place where the greatest under-development and socioeconomic problems exist. India, China, Pakistan, Bangladesh, and Indonesia presently account for half the increase in the world's population each year. Mexico contributes more to the total than the United States, Brazil more than the Soviet Union, the Philippines more than Japan—demonstrating clearly that smaller, less developed countries add more to net population growth than larger, developed countries.

I believe almost everyone today concedes that rational and moral population control is a desideratum of the highest priority, although there is obviously a great deal of disagreement as to the proper ways and means of control. Ideas range from strict government control by sterilization, abortion, and penalizing parents, to personal parental control by whatever means their consciences dictate. Then there is the actual poverty of available means of control. My own judgment is that because of inadequate research in the past, probably due to taboos and other cultural and religious factors, we know less about the biochemistry of human reproduction today than we do about the breeding of most farm animals.

As a member of the Rockefeller Foundation Board, I have constantly argued for a great increase of funding to the best centers of medical and biological research so that we might develop a whole new array of means, many of which I believe would meet any moral or cultural requirement imaginable. Moreover, I have argued against the "Fuller Brush" approach to population control whereby objectionable means of every variety are pushed upon large populations without the slightest regard for their cultural, religious, or psychological characteristics— the huckster approach, missionary in its fervor and insensitive in its methods. Naturally, most of these large target populations are poor, colored, or foreign; often the results are predictably short-lived and we are accused again of Yankee imperialism.

One current myth is that the Catholic church is the great obstructor of progress in this field. The simple fact is that developed or developing countries control their populations, and the less developed countries do not, irrespective of whether they are Catholic or not. Italy has the same low rate of population growth as

Sweden (doubling every eighty-eight years), and Spain the same low rate as Russia. Three predominantly Catholic countries, Paraguay, Ecuador, and Panama, have the same high rate of growth (doubling every twenty-one years) as three Moslem countries, Morocco, Syria, and Pakistan. I am not arguing the moral implications of these situations, although I would welcome some new inspirational, spiritual, and moral approaches to human sexuality, which has also been largely taken over by the hucksters. Here, I am simply citing the facts of the matter. Recent studies by the Overseas Development Council have shown that there is a constant factual correlation between human development and population control.

The conclusion is fairly obvious. If population control is a wise policy today, the surest road to its realization is greater concern for human development, especially where it is most needed: in the Southern Hemisphere of our planet. Most of what I will discuss in hopes of a better millennium to come will be in that interest.

But again, the present facts about population are ineluctable, whatever progress is made during the next decades in providing new, improved, humane, and moral controls. The next millennium will begin with between 6 and 7 billion people inhabiting this planet. The question remains: how will they be housed and fed, supplied with the necessary energy and natural resources for industrial processes, educated and politically organized for better human development and peace, assuming these to be our

goals in the next millennium? This question is all the
more poignant when one considers the present dismal
state of each of these aspects of man's development.
As a recent editorial of the *New Republic* stated of
Americans, "We are the social wastrels, spending
$2.7 billion a year on air-conditioning—roughly the
combined gross national products of Bolivia, Congo,
Liberia, Haiti and Guinea—while millions of our
aged lack proper care." * If we do so poorly, so
inequitably, so unjustly with 3.5 billion people, what
will we do with 6 or 7 billion having the same or even
heightened needs due to the revolution of rising
expectations? No easy question here.

There have been times when I have speculated that
the easiest way to solve the housing problems of
mankind would be to move the whole population of
the earth to the tropical zones where cold weather is
not a problem. Then I visited the sprawling slums of
Lagos, Nigeria, during a tropical rainfall and it was
clear that there are real shelter problems in the
tropics, too. The basic problem of housing is really
one of distributive justice. Everywhere in the world a
few people live in palaces—always have—and most
people live in shacks and shanties and cardboard or
wattle and mud huts. Again from the *New Republic*,
"The gospel of the marketplace is that the more we
consume the richer we are: waste and triviality equal
prosperity. Thus, we spend $6 to $8 billion on
cosmetics, toiletries and fragrances, and less than

* "Wastrel of the Western World," 170, nos. 1 & 2 (January, 1974): 6.

one-fifth that on subsidizing low-cost housing." *
And this in the United States, the richest country in
the world, a land of many palaces—where 6 million
present dwellings have been condemned as unfit for
human habitation. I have seen in most of our great
cities slum housing far worse than normal shelter for
farm animals. In other parts of the world, the quality
of housing goes lower and lower until one sees the
nadir in the less developed parts of Latin America,
Africa, and Asia. Here and there one sees bright new
housing schemes that seem to be working, as in
Singapore. But for most of humanity housing is costly
and money is scarce; so housing is a disaster,
unimaginably horrible to those Americans who have
seen the worst.

The present world housing problem, then, results
largely from the maldistribution of what is essential
to make human dignity at least a possibility. Another
contributing factor is a relatively new phenomenon
sweeping the whole world: urbanization. All the
world has witnessed the flight to the cities spurred by
the attraction of bright lights and the promise of
employment, the urban concentration of workers in
service and industrial enterprises, the downgrading of
farming as a way of life, massive refugee movements,
rising expectations of easy sudden wealth following
decolonization throughout Asia and Africa. More
than a third of mankind lives in cities, and the
prediction for the year 2000 is 60 percent. In the poor

* Ibid.

countries, the present urban population of 600 million is expected to grow to 3 billion by the next millennium. The population of cities of Latin America is doubling every fourteen years, with Rio, Sao Paulo, and Mexico City surpassing 7 million in population. I have seen the results in the swollen slums around Rio, Buenos Aires, Santiago, Lima, Caracas, Mexico City—where large proportions of whole national populations have flocked to the capital cities to seek a better life, only to find new misery. I have seen urbanization run wild in Africa and Asia. Calcutta and Bombay, Kinshasa and Lagos, Hong Kong and Saigon, Tokyo and Manila are disaster areas.

Even our own country, unusual because of its wealth, presents a typical example of the urbanization movement. For decades, a million families a year have been leaving the farms and flocking to the cities, with the result that today 75 percent of our population is living on 3 percent of our land. There is little rhyme or reason to this maldistribution of our living space, but we can hope for a better plan as we face the next millennium. Here again, we might set a good example. New cities are being pioneered in Britain, and great cities such as Sydney, Melbourne, and Adelaide were well planned from the beginning in Australia, a land as large as ours with a population equal to that of New York City. Here in America we are experimenting with new cities like Columbia, Maryland, and Reston, Virginia, where all socioeconomic classes and races are integrated in a situation that is both functional and beautiful. Open housing must be part of the pattern for the future if we are to solve the race problem and achieve integrated education and living.

For the larger answer, the key elements for the next millennium must be dispersal and rapid public transit. Cities are important to civilization as centers for education, culture, commerce, and government. The problem is that we have overburdened our cities, making them living rather than working and leisure spaces, allowing slums to fester and spread.

At present all who are able flee the city, and it further deteriorates, with a shrunken tax base and growing social difficulties. To compound the problem, industry is now also moving to the suburbs, where the poor, especially the minorities needing the jobs, cannot move because of restrictive and high-cost housing in the suburbs. So they are disproportionately out of work and the problems of poverty and consequent crime are compounded.

We need a completely new scheme. My only suggestion would be the removal of slums and the dispersion of most of its housing to open areas beyond the city. The city—all cities—need a complete overhaul of facilities, both educational and cultural, including parks, museums, and libraries. Around each great city, to a distance of a hundred miles or so, rapid transit facilities could move people from where they could live graciously to where they work, in a matter of half an hour or so—if only we abandon the one car, one person concept that so clogs our highways and pollutes our air and wastes our energy.

If the Japanese can move trains at 120 miles an hour, and I have enjoyed lunch at that speed without spilling my coffee, so can we and other countries. How to finance all of this? The *New Republic* reports, "The kitchen towel, usable again and again, may soon become obsolete: about a third of a billion dollars a year are spent on paper towels for the home. Place alongside that figure $232 million in federal cash outlays in fiscal '72 for urban mass transportation." * Clearly, the question is one of priorities. Ten cents additional gasoline tax would net ten billion additional dollars a year here in America; twenty cents, twenty billion. Even with presently rising prices, our gasoline costs only half as much as Europe's. Funds raised by such taxes could be earmarked for public transportation, rather than more roads. Priorities.

In any event we cannot continue to allow cities to decay and watch all civility die out in the process. The rest of the world's housing problem is far worse than ours and will probably need far more governmental intervention and planning, as has worked so well in Singapore. Our problem is more manageable, even though the Nixon administration has removed federal subsidies to housing, and we should therefore serve as leaders in correcting it. I predict that we will begin to handle this problem better as the new

* Ibid.

millennium approaches, simply because it cannot continue as it is—a truly national disgrace.

I want now to speak about food, not because I believe that man lives by bread alone, but because in the matter of human development I have always been impressed by that wonderful earthly wisdom of St. Teresa of Avila. She said, "If a hungry man asks you to teach him how to pray, you had better feed him first." And with all due respect to this ancient Christian tradition of giving bread to the hungry, I have been further impressed by Ghandi's wisdom in saying, "Give me a fish and I will eat today. Teach me how to fish and I will eat every day."

Food has been a perennial problem for mankind. We link the Eskimo with the seal and the salmon, the Sioux with the buffalo, the Inca with potatoes, the Mexican with corn and beans, the Oriental with rice, the tropical African with cassava or manioc. I should add in jest—although it is a bit of black humor—the American with hamburgers. Even though we raise more beef than any other country, we import one third of all the beef produced by the rest of them, which is really saying something in a largely hungry world. On the other hand, we have been generous with food grains from our surplus, which is now largely depleted because of Russian and Chinese demands and drought disasters around the world, especially in India and Africa. This should caution against the myth that America can feed the world. We have had a working buffer of 60 million acres of

agricultural land, not the best, sometimes all in use
when needed and other times in reserve when stocks
are high. That is the only buffer there has been, and
we are now using most of this acreage. World
demand for food has increased by 50 percent, while
current reserve food stocks worldwide are the lowest
they have been in twenty years. A few more natural
disasters and we may find it difficult to provide help.

This past summer, I visited the drought and famine
areas of three Sahelian countries, Senegal, Mauri-
tania, and Mali. I looked into the faces of hungry
men, women, and children living on the edge of the
desert. After four years of practically no rainfall their
animals had all died, depriving them of milk and
meat and their whole nomadic way of life. Here one
learns that behind the dismal statistics there is a
human condition that demands a solution. We were
flying into Timbuktu and Gao fifteen tons of food
grains per airplane each day, with three airplanes
available. This is the eyedropper approach to the
plight of hundreds of thousands of people, minimally
effective, but underlining the crying need for a better
long range solution. There are few sights more
heartrending than human beings without food or
drink. One understands, in seeing them, the premium
the good Lord placed on feeding the hungry and
giving drink to the thirsty. We must respond in a
more long range manner than these risky C-130
flights responding to cyclical crises.

The largest question regarding food is how we can
feed a world with hundreds of millions presently

undernourished and 5 million additional people to be fed each month. I believe there are two basic answers, apart from what we have already said about population control. The first answer is the green revolution: better genetic stocks of seed for higher productivity, better nutritional quality in all human food stuffs, and, of course, better animal and fish production for protein. The second answer is more land for agriculture. One thing is certain. Granting a population of 6 to 7 billion people in the year 2000, food production will at least have to double in the next three decades the total annual production achieved since the beginning of formal agriculture 10,000 years ago—and this would only sustain the present nutritional levels, which are insufficient for two thirds of the world's population.

My knowledge of the green revolution comes primarily from observing the great agricultural programs of the Rockefeller, Ford, and Kellogg Foundations, as well as the governmental aid programs that have now joined them in their worldwide efforts. Perhaps the best example of what private initiative and a few well-spent dollars can produce is the rice program. A little over a decade ago, the Rockefeller and Ford Foundations decided to support some serious rice research. Rice has been the staple food throughout the Orient for thousands of years, but no thorough research had ever been done on it. The foundations decided to make this an international project, governed by a board made up of plant and rice scientists from all over the Orient. The Interna-

tional Rice Research Institute was located at Los
Baños, outside Manila. I have been there three times,
and never cease to wonder at what has been accom-
plished in so short a time, and at such relatively low
price (at the same cost as a few supersonic military
aircraft).

Every known species of rice—there are over
10,000—was gathered, classified, and stored. Some
250 of the best species were identified according to a
check list of about thirty qualities, ranging from
reaction to fertilizers during growth to taste and
nutritional value. The better species were genetically
crossed to get one of the best. New fertilizers were
devised that could be sparingly used, to reduce cost
to the poor farmer. The stem borer, a rice pest, used
to be attacked by spraying insecticides, but the first
rainfall washed it off the plants. IRRI devised a new
systemic insecticide to be put into the irrigation
water, picked up by the root system, and deposited
throughout the plant so that the moths are killed
before the larvae can be laid to eat out the lymphatic
system. The meter high stems of the better rice
varieties like peta from Taiwan used to lodge—to
bend over—so that rats would eat large quantities
before it could be harvested. They also received less
sunlight while lodging. Genetically, the stem was
shortened to about half a meter, and a simple
electrified short chicken wire fence was devised to
eliminate the rats. Robert Chandler, the founder and
first director of IRRI, told me that the first harvest of
their first improved variety, IRRI-8, using the same

land and the same farmers, delivered a crop $1.3 billion more valuable than the year previous. The next year's crop made an advance of over 3 billion dollars. There have been at least four additional improved varieties since then. Between 1966 and 1970, the amount of land on which new varieties of rice and wheat were planted, mainly in Asia, grew from 41 thousand to almost 44 million acres, with spectacular results. The new millennium must see much more of this kind of imaginative, highly scientific approach to agriculture.

Following the success of IRRI, and an earlier success during the forties with hybrid corn in Mexico, under the leadership of Dr. George Harrar (subsequently president of the Rockefeller Foundation), there has been established a whole network of research stations in tropical agriculture at El Baton in Mexico, Centro International de Mejoramiento de Maiz y Trigo (CIMMYT), Centro International de Agricoltura Tropical (CIAT) at Palmyra, in the Cuaca Valley of Colombia; International Institute for Tropical Agriculture (IITA) at Ibadan in Nigeria; International Crop Research Institute for Semi-Arid Tropics (ICRISAT) in Hyderabad, India; a potato center in Peru. All of these centers interact and most of them have satellite or field stations in different climatic situations. When I visited the field station at Toluca, outside Mexico City, the plant breeder explained that each promising strain of seed goes through at least seven plantings, first to establish resistance to disease, and then to increase productivity. Samples are sent to eighty different counties for experimental planting under different conditions of climate and crop disease. There is a constant effort at improvement so that the world does not get locked into a monoculture.

There is also a concern in these centers not just for bigger and more disease-resisting crops, but for better food products from the standpoint of protein, amino acids, and vitamins. For example, in 1963 Edwin Mertz and his Purdue associates discovered a high lysine gene called Opaque-2 lost when hybrid corn was developed. When the gene was reintroduced, the corn had several times more vegetable protein than before. I saw a litter of pigs in Colombia, half of whom had been fed regular corn and half Opaque-2 corn. The latter half of the litter was, after three months of feeding, twice the size of the former. It is now hoped that a similar gene may be identified for the other food grains. In October 1972, Purdue scientists, after screening nine thousand varieties of sorghum, found two Ethiopian strains with a high lysine gene that will almost triple the protein quality of normal sorghum strains.

The world is in large part protein starved. When properly balanced, vegetable protein is a perfect substitute for animal protein. There are also new approaches to animal protein, such as planting *tilapia,* a milk fish, in the irrigated rice fields where it could be harvested with the rice. Hundreds of millions of tons of additional protein could be obtained this way, and in the lands where it is most needed. This is one more example of an unorthodox solution to an old problem.

Recent research has shown that early nutritional deficiency in the child results in poor brain development and damage to the central nervous system. By age one and a half, a child has all the brain cells he will ever have. Some poor Indian children get only about 500 calories a day during the first five years of life. Wherever this is happening, we are diminishing human mental capacity irreparably. One would hope that adequate nutrition for every human would be the minimal, essential goal for this whole planet during the next millennium. It is possible to conquer hunger, but agriculture must begin to have a higher priority and greater support than armaments. When children are diminished in their essential human capacity and the development of mankind is weakened, what is there left to defend?

I would insist on the necessity of massive action, fully supported by the governments involved, even when pioneered by private initiative, as most of the above projects were. The study to emphasize the need for tropical agriculture research was done by the National Academy of Sciences with government support. Four hundred and fifty scientific man years were spent in the effort. Their report was superb scientifically, but absurd politically, and thus abandoned by the government. A handful of us, under the leadership of Harrison Brown, international vice-president of the academy, and George Harrar of the Rockefeller Foundation, put the project back on the track, initiated it with Foundation money, and now several governments are supporting it, including our own and those of Canada, Great Britain, and Germany.

The effectiveness of these programs is impressive when massive effort is involved. Several of us were involved in West Pakistan's food plight some years ago, under the leadership of President Kennedy's science advisor, Jerome Wiesner (now president of M.I.T.). We were all so busy we could only meet and work at the White House on Sundays. Forty-two thousand tons of seed from the new short-stemmed durum wheat developed at the center in Mexico were shipped to West Pakistan. Four years later, Pakistan's problem was where to store the surplus wheat the new seed had produced.

I have gone into this detail to suggest what is possible if our leaders, especially in the less developed countries, begin to understand that agriculture is initially more important than steel mills, national jet air lines, and military establishments. Hungry and undernourished people simply lack the energy to build a nation, even to live a human life or plan a better one.

But the problem is far from being solved on a technical level, whatever the progress made in the cultivation of rice, wheat, corn, millet, sorghum, potatoes, yucca, cassava, and the genetic improvement of animal herds. This is an economic, as well as an agricultural problem, involving land tenure and the scientific study of the best land usage, credit, marketing, housing, and a wide variety of allied concerns. I would hope that the larger less developed countries might do in macrocosm what the small island of Formosa has done in microcosm through their Joint Council on Rural Reconstruction. This is a spectacular project, applying new economic and technical insights in small farmer community centers, where education and health care are available as well. India has attempted something of the same with considerable, though more limited, success because of its size and recent droughts. Latin America, Africa, and many parts of Asia could well emulate the J.C.R.R. of Formosa in the next millennium, but they should begin tomorrow.

Even if we could perfect agriculture to the nth degree, the new millennium would still face, with a growing population—even growing at a slower rate— the prospect of running out of arable land for food crops and grazing land for herds. There are a few great tracts left, like the llanos beyond the mountains in Colombia and Venezuela. The Amazon basin is enormous, but the soil is thin and leaches quickly when the tropical forest is removed. Argentina is a magnificent land, though underpopulated, and without any real growth in agricultural productivity during the last fifty years. On the other hand, countries like Bangladesh have an impossible density of population. The new millennium will certainly see the opening up of what few untouched or underpopulated areas there are on this planet; nevertheless, in order to feed well the world's population, we will

have to face the challenge of raising food in the
oceans that cover the largest part of the earth's
surface and of recovering for agriculture the third of
our total land mass classified as desert, lost to
agriculture entirely, although it has much good soil
and sunlight year round, lacking only water.

During one of the general conferences of the
International Atomic Energy Agency in Vienna, I
heard Alvin Weinberg, director of the U.S. Oak
Ridge National Laboratory, outline a plan that could
recover for agriculture and agricultural industry all of
these arid lands. This could be one of the major
projects of the new millennium: an enhancement of
earth's resources that will undoubtedly be needed if
we are to feed and employ twice the number of
people now living. The plan involves the use of
fast-breeder nuclear reactors for electrical energy
production and water desalination. Weinberg bases
the economy of the project on massive size and the
fact that the fast-breeder produces 400 megawatts of
electricity and 250 million gallons of water a day—
more fuel than it consumes. Using the cheap electricity to power about ten chemical industries around the
power plant, including the production of fertilizer,
would make the use of electricity to pump water to
the fields economically feasible. The new drip-
method underground irrigation system pioneered in
Israel uses only 60 percent as much water as open-
ditch irrigation, and would avoid the plague of
schistosomiasis that is afflicting the great irrigation
project associated with the Aswan Dam in Egypt and

the Volta in Ghana. Two of these reactors would open up fifteen hundred square miles of desert land to agriculture. Fortunately, many of our great deserts are adjacent to salt water in abundance—the Sahara in North Africa, the Atacama in Chile and Peru, and the great northern Australian desert, to mention a few.

I do not underestimate the difficulty involved in perfecting great fast-breeder reactors and reducing the cost of desalinating water, but under the impulse of the energy and food crises, I am convinced that it will be done by the next millennium. Meanwhile, we are learning more about arid-lands agriculture through ongoing projects at Puerto Penasco, Sonora, Mexico, and at Sadiyat in the sheikdom of Abu Dhabi on the Arabian Peninsula, both of which were initiated by the University of Arizona. The latter project, involving a hundred acres enclosed by fiber glass and polyethylene plastic, is already producing a ton of produce a day: cucumbers, eggplants, tomatoes, turnips. Cost is still a limiting factor in these projects, since they are using oil diesels for desalination. Weinberg's scheme would ultimately be more viable, but will profit by the arid land agricultural techniques now being pioneered in the smaller projects.

There is a political aspect to all of this that is not insubstantial in looking ahead. Formerly, power plants had to be placed near the sources of fossil fuels or water power. Nuclear plants carry their own fuel and, in the case of fast-breeders, produce additional fuel. Should the thermonuclear reaction of hydrogen fusion ever be harnessed, electrical power would be practically free. I would predict that this is still a long way off, however, because of the 100 million degree temperatures involved. But even nuclear fission reactors can be placed anywhere politically expedient and helpful.

When I first heard Weinberg's scheme, I thought of a use that would certainly be politically expedient. Apart from territorial considerations and senseless hates, the great bone of contention today between the Arabs and the Israeli is the presence of the million Palestinian refugees. As the Arabs and Israeli continue to talk, as they may for a long time, the Palestinians can be counted upon to cause crises—a Munich or a Khartum—to draw attention to their still unsettled plight. Now, after the Yom Kippur war, the Geneva conference for peace will be complicated by the Palestinian question. Until this inhumane condition is settled, the problem solved to everyone's satisfaction, it will continue to exacerbate the situation.

But suppose there were created in an Arab country—Egypt or Jordan—and in Israel these large installations, both feeding into a common electrical and water grid, to open up hundreds of thousands of acres in the now useless Sinai for year-round agriculture. Suppose that Palestinians were given first choice of this land—land far more productive than that of the West Jordan—with proper credit arrangements, twice as much land as each family lost, and special provision for children born in exile since the first Arab-Israeli war. One could not force Palestinians to take this land, but at least it would be available where none is now. The whole project could be placed under the control of the International Atomic Energy Agency and could be financed internationally. If successful, it would not only be a large step toward peace, but it would be an enormous pilot project for the next millennium's need for additional agricultural land. By way of postscript, similar large-scale projects would be a natural and normal investment outlet for the huge sums now being generated from the sale of Middle Eastern oil. It would seem both plausible and profitable to reinvest some of these monies in the area that generated them and which is still in dire need of development in modern agriculture, education, housing, and health care.

This area was the cradle of civilization. In the Middle Ages Arabs and Jews, particularly Avicenna and Averroes, kept alive the ancient wisdom of the Greek philosophers, promoting mathematics, architecture, astronomy, and medicine—and bringing all of this to an intellectually decadent Europe. The Middle East might yet become a cradle of revived culture if the constant threat of war and the flood of verbal hatred is replaced by a common endeavor for peace and justice by all Semitic peoples. Providing food may seem to be a banal approach to such a lofty dream, but people have often learned to cooperate when survival was at stake, and there will be fewer worldwide endeavors more related to survival on earth in the new millennium than the adequate production of food for all its inhabitants.

5 Toward a Global Education

We now move to a somewhat higher plane. If men and women can achieve the basic necessities of life, food and shelter, it still remains a problem to make life human, beautiful, intellectually and morally satisfying. The preparation for this falls under the broad rubric of education, beginning with the rudimentary verbal skills of literacy and quantitative reasoning, and passing on to the sciences (natural, physical, and social), technology, law, medicine, theology, literature, music, dance, and drama—all that we subsume under the word culture, or more broadly, in its organized form, civilization. One might say that we already have most of this well in hand, but remember that there are over 300 million children today who have never been in a school and probably never will be. Despite all the efforts of UNESCO, the many governmental aid programs, and the overseas projects of the great foundations, there are more illiterates in the world today than there were a decade or two ago: probably a third of humanity. Unless we can devise some ingenious new plan, there will be an ever increasing number of illiterates during the next millennium.

If we are presently slipping backward, what of the future, with increasing numbers of children arriving each day? Faulkner said, when receiving the Nobel Prize for literature in Stockholm, that man will not simply perdure, he will prevail. This is a brave announcement, but not one that will automatically be fulfilled. Today less than half of the children in Latin America ever enter a schoolroom. The figure is worse in sub-Saharan Africa and vast regions of Asia. And the number of children involved will double between now and the year 2000. Further, the educational gap of this generation is the technological gap of the next, perpetuating the inevitable economic gap between rich and poor, educated and uneducated, developed and underdeveloped. As children grow up, the educational problem of this generation becomes the unemployment problem of the next.

I have spoken of children, but there are also hundreds of millions of adults who share a hunger for knowledge that matches their physical hunger for food. I remember flying from Tangier to Casablanca alongside a Tuareg who watched me read my breviary. Finally, he reached into his pack and brought out a copy of the Koran, which he pretended to read, turning the pages of Arabic script slowly and solemnly. When I finished, I asked him if he knew what he was reading. "Not really," he said, "but I know that it must be beautiful." When the stewardess handed out the entrance visas, I had to fill his out for him. "When were you born," I asked. "I don't really know," he said, "You just fill in something for me."

I had never before realized what a deprivation illiteracy must be. Teilhard de Chardin speaks of the noösphere, a vast envelope matching the biosphere that encircles our globe. The noösphere represents the total production of man's intelligence and creativity, the total human culture of the world. To be completely cut off from this most precious patrimony must be the most cruel deprivation of all, and it afflicts unnecessarily about a third of all people on earth. The saddest part is that it is likely to afflict an even greater portion in the millennium to come. But there is a way out of this dilemma—a way not possible twenty-five years ago, but quite possible today.

I do not believe the global educational problem is solvable by conventional means: the building of classrooms, even in remote areas, and the preparation of a vast army of teachers. Very affluent countries may continue to pursue education this way, but even we in America have, almost without realizing it, created a vast system of nonconventional continuing education that today serves to educate more people than the conventional system, ranging from kindergarten to the university. We have certainly come to the time when we need to entertain some new and creative thoughts about the total enterprise of education, especially as it affects the less developed countries, which will become comparatively less and less developed without some new system of education.

A whole series of unrelated instruments developed since World War II has given us a communication capacity hitherto impossible. These new inventions are television, synchronous satellites, computers with vast memory banks of magnetic tape and the capacity for instant retrieval of billions of individual items, systems for miniaturizing stored materials (the whole Bible can be recorded on a postage-stamp size card), instant xerographic copying, the SNAP system for miniaturized atomic power units in satellites, and, with this additional power, the capability of millions of channels aboard a satellite for receiving and transmitting, ultimately transmitting directly from satellite to television set without the intervention (and interference and control) of a central ground receiving station. There are other marvels to come, but these, with the exception of the elimination of the ground station, are already in being now—though as stated above, none of them existed twenty-five years ago. It is not difficult to see what a combination of these would mean in developing a whole new approach to world education.

Thanks to the space program, we are now capable of launching and maintaining in space three synchronous satellites. These could be located above the Equator at three positions equidistant from each other, five and one half earth's radii out from the earth (about 23,400 miles), and traveling just under escape velocity so that they would remain in exactly the same spot in relation to the earth's rotation. From these three satellites millions of television programs could be transmitted to any spot on earth.

Three educational data banks could also be launched, one below each satellite. These data banks, to oversimplify, would contain the noösphere. It would be contained in several world languages, although in some areas of knowledge, such as science, English would emerge, as is now happening, as the one world language. Courses would be organized and recorded for the data bank ranging from literacy in a world language to astrophysics, each taught by the very best teacher in the world in that field, with all of the best visual aids. I cannot remember a clearer lesson in my life than that about the trans-uranium elements from Glenn Seaborg, for he discovered and predicted most of them. No more would any great teacher, anywhere in the world, be lost to mankind. Had this been possible in an earlier age, we could now hear Einstein on relativity theory, Oppenheimer on physics, Lavoisier on chemistry, Shakespeare on drama, Galileo on astronomy, Copernicus on his new theory of the solar system, and Keppler, Descartes, Newton in mathematics—on and on though the arts and sciences. We could sit at the feet of all the great philosophers, theologians, novelists, poets, artists, and architects.

Schools are as good as their teachers. As one who has visited schools, colleges, universities the world over for many years—as a kind of busman's holiday during our vacation time and in connection with

Peace Corps and university projects under many auspices—I can assure you that the further one goes from the centers of development, the poorer are the schools and the more depressing the quality of teaching. At a certain point it becomes the blind leading the blind, going nowhere. Now the genius of television is that the greatest teachers in the world can teach everyone who can see or hear them. Worldwide educational television would mean that even the local apprentice teachers would be taught every time they supervised a class taught by a great teacher.

Nothing of human culture, no great teacher, would ever again be lost to anyone on earth who had access to a television set and a directory telling him the proper number to dial to inform the satellite to signal the computer to retrieve and transmit within seconds, back through the satellite, the proper program in the proper language to the person requesting it. Never again would it matter where the person desiring an education happened to be, whether in a remote Andean village, an oasis in the Sahara, a craggy outpost in the Hindu Kush range of Afghanistan, a remote Pacific island, or an Arctic igloo. Nor would it matter what kind of an education he or she wished to have. Whatever is a valid subject for education would be included in the ever-growing educational data bank and would be instantly available.

Think of what this would mean, first in the case of literacy. The remotest village would have its miniaturized atomic-powered television set with an apprentice teacher to operate it—no greatly complicated task—and to help the learners get started with elementary literacy and mathematics. Then there would be all the other lessons needed most in less developed countries around the world: special courses for adults in health, agriculture, sanitation, crop planning by region, marketing, child care, home economics, nutrition. One can easily visualize an international corps, not unlike the Peace Corps, to help organize the total endeavor and train local paraprofessionals to carry it on. These local guardians of the television could be trained further by television when needed as an additional aid in learning. Moreover, the sets could be equipped to reproduce materials from the tube, diagrams, charts, even whole books of every description.

One of the worst features of rural life is boredom and isolation, and most of the population of less developed countries lives reluctantly in rural areas. This is what fuels urbanization, with all its evils. The presence of music and drama and opera, sports and news, learning and entertainment, could bring the best features of the cities into remote areas and give them new life. There are great human values to be learned from primitive peoples in rural areas, as our American Peace Corps volunteers have often told me: peace they never knew in the hurly-burly of modern living, family values, hospitality—simple joys. Much of this is lost through urbanization. Remove boredom and isolation and lack of educational opportunity from the rural areas, and the trend toward movement away might be reversed, with a much better distribution of the earth's population on its available space.

High intelligence, character, and genius exist all over the world, almost at random, and much of this scarce human resource is lost to humanity for lack of educational opportunity. There was, for example, a poor youngster born in a small village in the mountain area of West Pakistan. Someone noticed his innate mathematical ability and sent him to a distant elementary school, where he indeed showed great promise. He was sent from there to a more distant high school and thence to Cambridge, England, to study under one of the greatest physicists of our time in the Cavendish Laboratory. Without such intervention, this man, still young, would today be herding sheep across the border from Kashmir. Instead he is directing the International Center for Theoretical Physics, which enrolls promising scientists from the less developed countries.

Another boy was indeed herding sheep, in a rugged area of Yugoslavia, when someone perceptive saw him whittling figures from stray pieces of wood. He apprenticed the boy to the local stone cutter, where he was again noticed by someone, who sent him to study with Rodin in Paris. At nineteen, he had his own showing of sculpture there and became world famous, beautifying the world throughout his life.

And one young man was brought to my attention by a Colombian priest, Monsignor Joachim Salcedo, who was operating a literacy program called Radio

Sutatenza for the isolated mountain-dwelling campesinos North and West of Bogota. He claimed to have taught 2 million illiterates to read and write by radio, and published a paper for them, *El Campesino*, to continue their education. He told me of this promising young man who had learned to read and write in one of the mountaintop radio schools. This young man eventually came to the University of Notre Dame where he studied electrical engineering. Later, he received a graduate degree in business from an Ivy League university. He is now greatly aiding the economic growth of his own country.

All three of these men might have been performing far below their talents had they not been noticed—a chance affair—and educated. The world would have been poorer by far. And thousands of such talented people are being wasted today simply because they lack this educational opportunity. No one happens to notice them and do something to send them on their way upward. Worldwide educational television, a kind of university of the world, would begin to fill this crucial gap by liberating intelligent and talented men and women to learn, develop their talents, and serve others. My three friends were fortunate. Many others are not. We cannot continue to let chance decide.

One immediate objection to any scheme is cost. But let me remind you that in our country, *Sesame Street* reached half the children between three and five years of age and rendered them semiliterate when they arrived in kindergarten two years later. The cost

was less than a penny per day per child reached. The
total scheme here presented for the world cost far less
than the total annual world budget for armaments,
$200 billion. I need not add that most armament
expenditures are dead capital, whereas there are few
investments more productive than education. The
alternatives to this scheme are growing world illiteracy, wasted talent, hopelessness in further development, frustration, violence, war. What are the cost of
these? More dead capital.

The cost of this project would also be far less than
the expense of building classrooms and providing
teachers for a billion people, if even it could be
done—and the fact is, with herculean efforts, we have
fallen far short of the goal. Wherever a television set
were, there would be a classroom: in a town hall,
under a tree, even in a church or temple—for truth
and learning are indeed godly. And wherever there is
a classroom where people really learn, there is new
hope and fulfillment. What we cannot afford is to let
these die.

An objection comes from the developed countries,
who fear this would interfere with their existing
systems of schools, colleges, and universities. I do not
think it would. The educational establishment, with
few exceptions, is presently too entrenched and too
conservative to make adequate use of the new
technology. That is why continuing education has
grown up largely outside the present formal systems
of education and has pioneered far more with
technological aids largely unused by conventional

education. There is much to be said for person-to-person education, but in the present world, there just are not enough logs and Mark Hopkinses, given the dire need in the less developed and largely illiterate parts of the world. UNESCO is already proposing a satellite plan for education in India, which is 70 percent illiterate, and which presently spends five dollars per student annually, one two-hundredth of the United States expenditures. Brazil and Indonesia are also interested. I would suggest, as one of our priority endeavors in approaching the new millennium, that we test the technique with one satellite and one data bank in the Western Hemisphere. I believe that with proper leadership and resources it will work, especially since we are dealing with a limited number of languages: Spanish and Portuguese in Central and South America, English and French in the North.

I should add here that I visualize this continental and world endeavor as a two-way street, not as another exercise in cultural imperialism. All parts of the world have much to learn from each other. The richness and variety of human culture should not be homogenized. All should have a say in what goes into the data bank and in what form. If it is successful, one would hope that the university of the world will eventually become a reality, and illiteracy a bad dream of times past.

There is yet another hurdle facing the full realization of the potential inherent in a university of the world. Even if the project could be financed, there is the political obstacle that has always been the enemy of universities anywhere, under whatever auspices. When universities began, in the Middle Ages, they were Catholic. The first and the greatest, founded in Paris in 1205, soon had to seek a papal charter to remove its faculty and students from the control of the local civil and church authorities. Ever since, universities have been struggling to maintain their academic freedom and autonomy. The 1965 general conference of the International Association of Universities, a UNESCO dependency, had for its general theme "The Freedom and Autonomy of the University." Despite all the rhetoric at the Tokyo meeting, it soon became obvious that whatever the auspices or geopolitical locations of the universities, they all were still struggling to maintain their freedom and autonomy against both external and internal pressures. Nor could a university of the world hope to escape the eternal tension between those who believe in intellectual freedom and those who do not.

I am reminded of a petty but powerful ruler whose subjects were grievously afflicted with trachoma and blindness. A friend of mine who had a large commercial interest in that country was struck with compassion at the sight of so many blind people, especially when the disease could be easily arrested by applying sulfa salve to the eyes. He obtained a million dollars and persuaded a drug company to prepare the drug in handy small capsules. When he told the ruler of his plan, this bully said, "Nothing doing. Leave my people alone. They're much easier to rule when they are half or fully blind."

This may well represent in parable form the reaction of the politically powerful of the world nations when they are confronted with the possibility of their people's free and open access to all knowledge—history and science, not to mention political theories or religious concepts other than their own, and understanding of cultural differences—and with hopes, new aspirations, and quickly rising expectations, perhaps for justice and equity and real human freedom in today's world. The same answer may be forthcoming: "Nothing doing. Leave my people alone. They are easier to rule when they are half or fully blind."

True development means the liberation of mankind to be truly human. The acid test of development in the next millennium may be whether or not political authorities will allow people to be truly free, to have access to what is known about politics, religion, culture, as well as a wide variety of other human realities that really liberate a man or woman. We faced the same dilemma in a smaller context when printing began and literacy spread throughout Europe. It is difficult to calculate the effect on rising expectations of the now almost omnipresent transistor radio. But we do know that attempts to jam programs were as massive as attempts to transmit them.

The Lord once said that the children of darkness

are wiser in their generation than the children of light. I caught a glimpse of this in a few sketchy news reports from Paris regarding a UNESCO board meeting that dealt with television communication. A rather harsh resolution was debated, to the effect that all satellite transmitted programs had to pass through a ground station and whether or not they were allowed to enter a particular country would be under the complete control of government authorities. That some countries were promoting this restriction was not surprising. My greater concern was that the delegates from more open countries—including our own—were not fighting for freedom. I said to myself, "There goes another great idea," another victory for the children of darkness, with the children of light asleep, as the Lord foretold.

It was not lost on totalitarian regimes that the new communications technology was enormously power-ful, especially in the realm of ideas. Our landing on the moon was televised worldwide and watched almost everywhere television was available (there are still some large countries holding the line against it). I remember standing in front of the first space photos of the moon walk shown in the window of the U.S. Information Service in Addis Ababa, Ethiopia. I was surrounded by a group of ragged little wide-eyed boys who did not know a word of English, but who were pointing to the pictures and yelling, as if in a cheer, "Armstrong, Neil Armstrong." I could not help but think that Venetian youngsters in a different age must have pointed to a man and said, "Polo,

Marco Polo," meaning that the world was not just Venice or even Europe. The moon walk inspired an instantaneous lifting of the human spirit everywhere, and live television brought it even to illiterate boys in far-off Addis Ababa.

I will not say more, except that the new millennium will see far greater and more widespread development of people in the truest sense—liberation of the human spirit through learning—if this new approach to worldwide education is indeed, as I believe it to be, an idea whose time has come. No politician or group of politicians should be allowed to obstruct this liberation. But the U.S. cannot promote education abroad simply by pumping in rhetoric, plans, or even money, if we do not in our own system set an example of what education can and should be. And in light of recent national scandals, some intensive reexamination is called for—not into our technical means of education, but into the uses to which we put its liberating capacity. Somewhere, in that vague morass of rhetoric that has always characterized descriptions of liberal education, one always finds a mention of values. The true purists insist on intellectual values, but there have always been educators, particularly among founders of small liberal arts colleges in the nineteenth century, who likewise stressed moral values as one of the finest fruits of their educational process, especially if their colleges were inspired by a religious group.

I believe it to be a fairly obvious fact that we have come full circle in our secularized times. Today one hears all too little of intellectual values, and moral values seem to have become a lost cause in the educational process. I know educators of some renown who practically tell their students, "We don't care what you do around here as long as you do it quietly, avoid blatant scandal, and don't give the institution a bad name."

Part of this attitude is an overreaction to *in loco parentis,* which goes from eschewing responsibility for students' lives to just not caring how they live. It is assumed that how students live has no relation to their education which is, in this view, solely an intellectual process. Those who espouse this view would not necessarily deny that values are important in life. They just do not think that they form part of the higher education endeavor if, indeed, they can be taught anyway.

Moral abdication or valuelessness seems to have become a sign of the times. One might well describe the illness of modern society and its schooling as *anomie,* a rootlessness. I would like to say right out that I do not consider this to be progress, however modern and stylish it might be. The Greeks (not the fraternities!) were at their best when they insisted that (*arete*) excellence, was at the heart of human activity at its noblest, certainly at the heart of education at its civilized best. John Gardner wrote a book on the subject that will best be remembered by his trenchant phrase: "Unless our philosophers and plumbers are committed to excellence, neither our pipes nor our arguments will hold water."

Do values really count in a liberal education? They have to count if you take the word "liberal" at its face value. To be liberal, an education must somehow liberate a person actually to be what every person is: free. Free to be and free to do. What?

Excuse me for making a list, but it is important. The first goal of a liberal education is to free a person from ignorance which fundamentally means freedom to think, clearly and logically. Moreover, allied with this release from stupidity—nonthinking or poor thinking—is the freedom to communicate one's thoughts, hopefully with clarity, style and grace, more than the Neanderthal grunt. A liberal education should also enable a person to judge, which in itself presupposes the ability to evaluate: to prefer this to that, to say this is good and that bad, or at least this is better than that. To evaluate is to prefer, to discriminate, to choose, and each of these actions presupposes a sense of values. Liberal education should also enable a person to situate himself or herself within a given culture, religion, race, sex, and, hopefully, to appreciate what is valuable in the given situation, even as simple an evaluation as "black is beautiful." This, too, is a value judgment and a liberation from valuelessness, insecurity and despair at times. Liberal education, by all of these value-laden processes, should confer a sense of peace, confidence and assurance on the person thus educated and liberate him or her from the adriftness that characterizes so many in an age of *anomie.*

Lastly, a liberal education should enable a person

to humanize everything that he or she touches in life, which is to say that one is enabled not only to evaluate what one is or does, but that, in addition, one adds value consciously to relationships that might otherwise be banal or superficial or meaningless: relations to God, to one's fellow men, to one's wife or husband or children, to one's associates, one's neighborhood, one's country and world.

In this way, the list of what one expects of liberal education is really a list of the very real values that alone can liberate a person from very real evils or nonvalues—stupidity, meaninglessness, inhumanity.

One might well ask at this juncture, "How are these values attained educationally?" Again, one is almost forced to make a list: language and mathematics stress clarity, precision, and style, if well taught; literature gives us insight into that vast human arena of good and evil, love and hate, peace and violence as real living human options. History gives a vital record of mankind's success and failure, hopes and fears, the heights and the depths of human endeavors pursued with either heroism or depravity —but always depicting real virtue or the lack of it. Music and art purvey a sense of beauty seen or heard, a value to be preferred to ugliness or cacophony. The physical sciences are a symphony of world order, so often unsuccessfully sought by law, but already achieved by creation, a model challenging man's freedom and creativity. The social sciences show man at work, theoretically and practically, creating his world. Too often, social scientists in their quest for a physical scientist's objectivity underrate the influence of freedom—for good or for evil. While a social scientist must remain objective within the givens of his observable data, his best contribution comes when he invokes the values that make the data more meaningful, as De Tocqueville does in commenting on the values of democracy in America, Barbara Ward in outlining the value of social justice in a very unjust world, Michael Harrington in commenting on the nonvalue of poverty. Again, it is the value judgments that ultimately bring the social sciences to life and make them meaningful in liberating those who study them in the course of a liberal education.

One might ask where the physical sciences liberate, but, even here, the bursting knowledge of the physical sciences is really power to liberate mankind: from hunger, from ignorance and superstition, from the grinding poverty and homelessness that have made millions of persons less than human. But the price of this liberation is value: the value to use the power of science for the humanization rather than the destruction of mankind.

Value is simply central to all that is liberalizing in liberal education. Without value, it would be impossible to visualize liberal education as all that is good, in both the intellectual and the moral order of human development and liberation. Along the same line of reasoning, Robben Fleming, president of the University of Michigan this year asked his faculty why, in the recent student revolution, it was the liberal arts

students who so easily reverted to violence, intoler-
ance and illiberality. Could it not be that their actions
demonstrated that liberal education has begun to fail
in that most important of its functions: to liberate
man from irrationality, valuelessness and *anomie?*

But, one might legitimately ask, how are these
great values transmitted in the process of liberal
education? All I have said thus far would indicate
that the values are inherent in the teaching of the
various disciplines that comprise a liberal education
in the traditional sense. However, one should admit
that it is quite possible to study all of these branches
of knowledge, including those that explicitly treat of
values, philosophy and theology, without emerging as
a person who is both imbued with and seized by great
liberating and humanizing values. I believe that all
that this says is that the key and central factor in
liberal education is the teacher-educator, his percep-
tion of his role, how he teaches, but, particularly, how
he lives and exemplifies the values inherent in what
he teaches. Values are exemplified better than they
are taught, which is to say that they are taught better
by exemplification than by words.

I have long believed that a Christian university is
worthless in our day unless it conveys to all who
study within it a deep sense of the dignity of the
human person, his nature and high destiny, his
opportunities for seeking justice in a very unjust
world, the inherent nobility so needing to be achieved
by each, for himself and for others, whatever the
obstacles. I would have to admit, even immodestly,

that whatever I have said on this subject has had a minuscule impression on those who have heard me, compared to what I have tried to do to achieve justice in our times. This really says that while value education is difficult, it is practically impossible unless the word is buttressed by the deed.

If this is true, it means that all those engaged in education today must look to themselves first, to their moral commitments, to their lives, and to their own values which, for better or worse, will be reflected in the lives and attitudes of those they seek to educate. There is nothing automatic about the liberal education tradition. It can die if not fostered. And if it does die, the values that sustain an individual and a nation, and indeed the world, are likely to die with it.

6   A Triregional World

This brings us to a consideration of the political alignment of the world in the next millennium. I am on thinner ice here, for because of the nature of my personal knowledge and experience, I am indulging more in speculation than in prediction based on firm evidence. Someone once remarked to Winston Churchill that Clement Attlee was a modest man. Churchill replied, "He has a lot to be modest about." In this context, so do I. A few words are necessary on this subject, however, since what happens regarding the political organization of the world will greatly affect all else I have predicted. At least I can speak in hope.

Recently I read Philip Hughes's *History of the Catholic Church.* While this is not a general history, it was helpful by way of perspective to view one institution that has coexisted with the first two millennia and is about to move into the third, enormously changed in the past decade because of Vatican Council II. I might add, changed for the better on most counts, as I view it, although it has happened so quickly that it has shaken a lot of people who need firm structures to lean on. Reading rapidly through two thousand years of change creates the impression that, in some spiritual, many material, and most scientific and technological ways, the world itself has changed more in the postwar era than in all of the past two millennia. That is a very large statement—one impossible to document fully—but I will mention a few examples. We have printed almost twice as many books since 1945 as in all the centuries since printing was invented by Gutenberg. I will not say we have doubled our wisdom, but knowledge has increased spectacularly, particularly in the sciences, more than doubling since the war. All through history man was limited to the speed of running fast or racing a horse, until at the turn of the century he achieved fifty miles an hour with the steam engine. In the next fifty years, he multiplied that speed ten times, fulfilling Admiral Byrd's prediction after flying the Atlantic at 90 mph in 1928 that man would probably reach 500 mph in the future. It was the very near future. In the period since the war, we have learned to move fifty times faster than 500 mph. The astronauts are going about 25,000 mph when they reenter the earth's atmosphere from the moon.

We have used in this postwar period more energy than mankind used from his advent on earth until World War II. We have taken a quantum step in energy production with the advent of the nuclear age and will take another when we learn to harness the

thermonuclear reaction, the source of all the energy
we receive from the sun.

We in America have tripled our higher educational
endeavor during the past twenty-five years, from the
3 million students of 1950—the highest point since
the beginning of American higher education with
Harvard's founding in 1636—to a new high of over 9
million students. Faculties and facilities have also
tripled. We did more by twice in twenty years than
had been done in the preceding three centuries.

One could go on and on, as Toffler does in *Future
Shock*, but this should suffice as a background for the
political change that occurred at the same time, and
with comparable rapidity, changing the political
premises held for centuries. Since the age of explora-
tion in the late fifteenth and sixteenth centuries, the
world had been politically accustomed to the regime
of European empires with their vast colonial holdings
in Asia, Africa, and earlier, in Latin America. Then
suddenly, following the cataclysmic Second World
War, Europe came apart at the seams. There was the
unusual historical fact of the United States, the most
militarily powerful and victorious state in history, not
wanting or taking an additional foot of territory after
the victory. Then there were the Four Freedoms—
freedom from want and fear, freedom of speech and
religion—an interesting constellation of hopes, not
unrelated to all we have been predicting for the new
millennium. People, especially colonial peoples, lis-
tened to that wartime proclamation of the Four
Freedoms and wanted them all, for themselves.

It took some time after the war for the movements of political liberation to jell. Even Winston Churchill said he did not become Prime Minister to dismember the British Empire. Now that it has happened, we tend to forget how recent it was. But I can remember attending the charter conference of the International Atomic Energy Agency at the United Nations in 1956. All nations were invited and most came, even the Vatican, which I represented with Marston Morse of the Institute for Advanced Studies at Princeton. There were only 47 nations in attendance—and that was only 17 years ago. At a similar conference today there would be at least 140 nations. I recall travelling throughout sub-Saharan Africa in 1958. At that time, of the longtime colonies only Ghana had become an independent nation. Today practically all are independent, with the exception of Portuguese Angola, Mozambique, and a few tiny Spanish enclaves.

It seems almost inevitable that all these peoples, including those on the vast Indian subcontinent, should have been liberated. It seems less a matter of rejoicing that nationalism, in all of its worst aspects, was reborn and reinvigorated in almost every new nation. This may be partially due to a reborn pride of the people in their cultures. That is certainly good. But it can be overdone too, especially in an ever more interdependent world.

As a result of all this, we have begun to see the impossibility of trying to govern a small planet like this, or maintain its peace, when votes are equally distributed to the very powerful and the very weak,

the very large and the very small. Whatever one says
of *Realpolitik*, there is something very unreal about
the geopolitical operation of the United Nations
today. So we have ineffective posturing, rhetoric in
five languages and millions of words. We have voting
by alignment rather than by what is right and just. A
small evil is loudly condemned here, and a massive
evil is conveniently overlooked there. It doesn't work
and must be overhauled before we can move politically with any confidence into the next millennium.

In the last analysis, it has been the great powers
that have called the tune during the past two and a
half decades—and the tune was "Cold War," with
not unrelated heatings in the Far East, in Korea, and
Vietnam. Fortunately, that seems to be coming to an
end, with the United States now on good terms with
China and Russia, though the latter two are still
mighty fidgety about each other. Europe has moved
toward economic unity and Japan is really booming,
with the third highest GNP in the world.

Now against this background, I will dare make my
speculations about the evolving shape and structure
of this new world, approaching the next millennium.

First, I would postulate that there will be a new
North–South orientation resulting largely in a triregional world. In the past, going back to the earliest
days of European trade with the Orient and the New
World, the important orientation was mainly East–
West. North–South represented trade of an exploitive
nature, picking up raw materials for low prices and
dumping cheap manufactured goods for higher

prices. The North became wealthy while the countries of the Southern hemispheres, Australia and New Zealand excepted (they were settled by Europeans) mainly remained poor. Even today the important political powers—the big five of the United States, Great Britain, France, USSR, and China, with Japan now added—are on an East–West axis.

With the decolonization of the world and the ridiculously large number of sovereign powers emerging, arranged at best by historical accident and at worst by wars, we realize that we must seek a better political structure for our small planet. I suggest that a triregional arrangement on a North–South orientation might develop in something like the following sequence: Japan and China are emerging as the great powers in the Orient, especially as the United States withdraws. Russia will be squeezed out or neutralized, driving it and its satellites into much closer cooperation with a unified Europe (Russia in the process conveniently finding itself more European than Oriental anyway). The total economy of the Orient will loom large, especially if you consider the potential mineral wealth of Indonesia, Malaysia, and western Australia. Japan is already ranked third economically in the world, even without this total North–South alliance in the Orient.

The whole emerging European Economic Community, plus Russia and the satellite countries, will vie with the Orient for economic first place. The present E.E.C., without all its potential partners, will attain 80 percent of the level of the United States GNP by

1980. Once the potential community is totally organized and looks south to the Middle East and Africa, it does not take much imagination to see the United States in third place. If this begins to happen, and it well might, our natural region, largely neglected by us thus far, is the Western Hemisphere: Canada and Latin America. We are already about as close to Canada economically as can be, perhaps too close for their liking. To the south, there have been regional stirrings in Central America and in the Andean region. Brazil is by all odds the new leader of the third world, as was evident at the 1972 United Nations Trade and Development Conference in Santiago, Chile, and at the Stockholm World Environmental Conference a few months later. The United States will have an enormous fence-mending task to do before anything like an economic community of the Western Hemisphere can be evolved. If my speculations are anywhere near the mark, we had best begin the mending.

Others may have a better scenario for what is evolving in the political structure of the world as the millennium approaches. Certainly, three strong and equally powerful North–South regions would seem to be geographically rational and would make the political structure of this small planet more reasonable, more amenable to peace, even more just. The North–South alignment could be greatly conducive to development, with a better distribution of the finite resources of the earth. Each center of economic strength in the North would be related to a large southern area of present economic weakness, but great potential development. Such a North–South orientation would not prevent normal East–West trade continuation, but arrangements for tariff or free trade could be negotiated among regional communities, without the strong preying on the weak. Moreover, the best trade and credit benefits could be within each of the three regional communities themselves for their internal health and growth.

As Lester Brown has observed in *World Without Borders*, a book that has provided me with many statistics,

> In effect, our world today is in reality two worlds, one rich, one poor; one literate, one largely illiterate; one industrial and urban, one agrarian and rural; one overfed and overweight, one hungry and malnourished; one affluent and consumption-oriented, one poverty-stricken and survival-oriented. North of this line, life expectancy at birth closely approaches the biblical threescore and ten; South of it, many do not survive infancy. In the North, economic opportunities are plentiful and social mobility is high. In the South, economic opportunities are scarce and societies are rigidly stratified.*

One might add that the gap is continually widening, and will continue to do so unless something like I suggest begins to happen.

* *World Without Borders* (New York: Random House, 1972), p. 41.

To illustrate this from the most recent energy crisis: while one hears loud cries of anguish from the developed world, the increased costs for the underdeveloped world next year will be, because of rising prices, $10 billion additional for fuel and $5 billion additional for food. This is six times greater than the total present annual aid to these countries from the United States. India's costs for fuel and food will rise from $2.5 to $4 billion—and there is a serious question where the food will come from in today's depleted market. To add to the crisis, Japan has decided to cut its fertilizer program, on which much of Asia depends, rather than the manufacture of automobiles for export to the rich countries.

I have consciously drifted from politics to economics; now back to my original political speculations again. Brown adds (on p. 157) in his book a quote from Robert McNamara of the World Bank: "The outlook for the seventies is that the fault line along which shocks to world stability travel will shift from an East–West axis to a North–South axis, and the shocks themselves will be significantly less military and substantially more political, social, and economic in character." Somehow men and nations act more quickly and more decisively under economic than under political necessity. That economic necessity—one of the "shocks" of which McNamara speaks—whether viewed as a crisis of global development, peace, monetary systems, trade, or energy, is already upon us. The emerging crises are shaping history in a wide variety of ways. I believe that political community, or regional groupings, will follow the economic realities. Already the Cold War terminology of three worlds, one democratic, one socialistic, and one nonaligned and poor, is out of date. There are not really three worlds today, but two—the developed and the underdeveloped, the rich and the poor, the North and the South. A triregional alignment of these two worlds may be the best promise of the new millennium.

If this should happen, we would see a vastly different economic and political world. Many of the hopes I have already enunciated would be greatly facilitated by such a new triregional community. In proposing all this, I continue to see regional economics and politics as subordinate to the common good of the human community. But creative economics and creative politics are an important part of man's creative force in human history as we try to create a new vision of earth and man, liberated from the alienations, exploitations, indignities, hatreds, and violence of the past.

All that has been said thus far has been woven with the common thread of human development. The concept of development was pioneered by Schumpeter, who used the German term *Entwicklung* perhaps more in the sense of *evolving*. Those who first developed the concept, and many yet today, such as Paul Samuelson and W. W. Rostow, speak of development mainly in the economic sense. With so much underdevelopment in the world today—witness the

1.9 billion people who make less than $100 a year—
no wonder economics has been called the gloomy
science. Again, as Lester Brown said so well, "An
affluent global minority is overfed and overweight,
but more than half of humanity is hungry and
malnourished; some can afford heart transplants, but
half of humanity receives no health care at all; a
handful of Americans have journeyed to the moon,
but much of mankind cannot afford a visit to the
nearest city; several thousand dollars are spent on a
college education for a young American, while much
of mankind lacks the limited resources required to
become literate. In a shrinking world, these growing
disparities place great stress on the international
political fabric." *

But over time, and as scholars became more
involved in the actual work of development, going
beyond models to the realities (as I once saw Walter
Rostow wrestling with realities in Latin America
together with the seven "wise men" of the Organization of American States), it became more and more
evident that development must be thought of as a
total process—"integral development" as Paul VI
used the term in his best encyclical, *Populorum
Progressio.* It is in this sense that I have attempted to
use the concept of human development in looking
ahead to the year 2000. Man's religious and moral
consciousness is deeply involved, as well as his
physical and intellectual well being; it too is touched
by his sustenance and educational opportunities.

* Ibid., p. 9.

Having underlined all of this, and having made a whole spate of hopeful predictions, I should add that the people of the Third World, which has during the Cold War languished between the capitalistic and socialistic world, are increasingly having thoughts of their own regarding their own development. Some of them, especially in Latin America, do not even like the sound of the word *development* (*desarrollo* for them) because it has had so many overtones of dependency upon those who are already developed. Perhaps this dependency is inevitable, as development does require capital, credit, technical assistance, experts, and a host of other means. However, Latin Americans argue, much of the development thus far has been a one-way street: they have had to accept our model of development so that while they go ever more deeply into debt, their iniquitous feudal social structures remain largely untouched, the rich getting richer and the poor poorer. What the new breed in Latin America want is a change of concept, substituting the word *liberation* for *development.* They want this, negatively, to eliminate the connotation of dependency, and, positively, to be freed to work out their own plans for liberating those large masses of the dispossessed from their grinding poverty, misery, alienation, exploitation, and indignity.

I am using the words they use, and it would be honest to add that many of the younger revolutionary elements are more attracted by socialism than they are by capitalism, which they regard as their ancient despoiler. That is why people like Che Guevara,

Camilo Torres, and even Fidel Castro are more idealized than Nixon, Wilson, or even Willie Brandt. While I am not arguing their case, which often appears to people from developed countries to be naïve, subversive, ungrateful, or just plain foolish, I understand their frustration. Capitalism has dealt more brutally with them than it has with our own poor and racial minorities. Certainly, they should be allowed to determine their own destiny, even make their own mistakes, especially in choosing their own model of development, whether or not it comes out looking more like socialism than capitalism. I believe that we can work with them on their terms and not always and everywhere completely on our terms, according to our plans for them.

The Chinese, for example, have developed in extraordinary ways, by themselves, mainly without foreign aid. We may not like the Russians being communists either, but in point of fact, they were an oppressed society, 97 percent illiterate, before the revolution, whereas they are highly developed educationally today. Perhaps none of us would like to pay the price of freedom that both the Chinese and the Russians paid, but we can believe strongly in our own model for development while coexisting with and even helping others having a different model. This should not be an impossible stance when the Republicans can get the American taxpayers to subsidize wheat for Russia at a cost of $300 million, getting higher food prices here in the process.

The real reason we are willing to give more leeway

to Russia and China is because we respect their power, while we tend to patronize Latin Americans and Africans as powerless, undisciplined poor. If what I have previously said about our own future being closely interwoven with the future of the Western Hemisphere makes any sense, then we had better find another Henry Kissinger who is as interested in our underdeveloped neighbors, as the real Henry Kissinger is effectively interested in our powerful erstwhile enemies. The Third World will not go away; in fact it has much that we need and want. But especially the massive Latin American segment of the Third World, which will number over 600 million people by the end of the century, and to whom we have been both a good and a bad neighbor, deserves something uniformly better in the next millennium: first, greater understanding from us in the sense that they call *sentimiento* and, second, a two-way traffic that makes for a better hemisphere, and also a better world, whether we call it development, liberation, or both.

I had hoped that, as was originally proposed, the 1973 U.S. foreign aid bill would be entitled "Mutual Development and Cooperation," along with the agency that was to carry out the bill's provisions—one of which was to establish a billion dollar credit annually for that poorest 1.9 billion of the world's people. Unfortunately, the new title was scuttled in the congressional conference committee and the new form of aid in the House of Representatives. We should be reminded occasionally that we have about as much trade with the developing nations as we do with the whole European Economic Community and Japan combined. If the new provision of this aid bill had been enacted, we would probably be doing more trade with the least developed, which has been largely untouched by former programs. But this important point is lost on those with tunnel vision.*

I can, however, think of better motives for helping our needy neighbors than those just mentioned. I hope that these better, more altruistic motives will be more apparent in the concluding section.

* Recently, Congress refused to replenish the funds we had promised for the World Bank's soft loan window, which is the best hope of the poorest in the developing countries.

7 Citizens of the World

The most stirring photograph brought back from the moon by the astronauts was a faraway picture of the earth itself. There it shines as no earth dweller had ever seen it before: blue, flecked with white cloud patterns, a beautiful small globe set against the black void of space through which it is whirling at incredible speed. Archibald MacLeish caught the poetry of the vision. It is up to all of us to make it come true.

The sad reality is that the earth is much more beautiful from afar than it is up close. Not that physical beauty does not exist on earth. I have been awed by the majesty of the soaring, snowy, wind-swept heights of the Himalayas seen against the jade green uplands of Nepal. The pastel-colored sweep of the Britannica Range in Antarctica seen from McMurdo base camp almost two hundred miles away is enough to thrill the soul of any observer. A sunset following a storm at sea, a sunrise on the hushed African game-filled caldera of Ngorongoro Crater, the Cordillera Blanca of Peru and Chile viewed from a high flying jet on a bright winter afternoon, these are unforgettably beautiful earthly visions. Note, though, that in most of them man, apart from the viewer, is almost completely absent, and where man is present in large numbers on earth, one can almost always expect a diminution of beauty—both physical beauty, diminished through pollution, and spiritual beauty, marred by violence and injustice.

It is a singular blessing for our age that we have been able to see the earth from the moon, to see it as it really is, in Barbara Ward's words: Spaceship Earth, a beautiful, small space vehicle, providing a viable ecosystem for human beings, but with quite limited resources.* As Heilbroner said so well, "Life on this planet is a fragile affair, the kind of miraculous microbial activity that flourished on the thin film of air and water and decomposed rock which separates the uninhabitable core of the earth from the void of space." † We, the passengers of Spaceship Earth, are capable of creating by our intelligence and freedom a whole series of man-made systems that will enhance the inherent beauty of our planet and make it even more humanly viable. Or we can turn Spaceship Earth into an ugly wasteland where human beings barely survive and hardly live in any human sense.

If you have any doubt that we are doing the latter rather than the former, walk through the streets of

* *Spaceship Earth* (New York: Columbia University Press, 1966).
† "Growth and Survival," *Foreign Affairs* 51, no. 1 (October, 1972): 139.

Calcutta, visit the favelas, barriadas, villas miserias, and callampas surrounding the Latin American capital cities, step aboard the floating junks adjacent to Hong Kong's harbor, look at the native locations north of Johannesburg in South Africa, or inspect some of America's own inner city slums, Chicano colonias in the Southwest, or miners' rotting villages in Appalachia, or almost any American Indian reservation in the West. It isn't just what you see that will sicken you. It is that it is all so unnecessary, that it is man-made and man-kept, and that it is in startling contrast to the way other humans are living in luxury only a few miles away from each of these human sewers and garbage heaps.

An easy answer would be to say that there are just not enough of the world's resources to house and feed everyone. But then remember that last year, and for most of the years we can remember, the governments of this planet have spent more than $200 billion on armaments—and that is more than the total annual income of the poorest half of the earth's population. We do it because the Russians do it, and they do it because we do it, and so the foolishness goes on and on and on, all around the world. Meanwhile, the poor go to bed hungry, when they are lucky enough to have beds.

To put the case for the poor most simply, imagine our Spaceship Earth with only five people aboard instead of more than 3.5 billion. Imagine that one of those five crew members represents those of us earth

passengers who live in the Western world of North
America and Europe—one-fifth of humanity on
earth, mainly white and Christian. The person representing us has the use and control of 80 percent of the
total life-sustaining resources available aboard our
spacecraft. The other four crewmen, representing the
other four-fifths of humanity—better than 2.5 billion
people—have to get along on the 20 percent of the
resources that are left, leaving them each about 5
percent to our man's 80 percent. To make it worse,
our man is in the process of increasing his portion of
these limited resources to 90 percent.

Now if this sounds piggish to you, it is! If you
speak of resources just in terms of energy, which is
popular today, we in the United States, with 6
percent of the world's population, used last year
about 40 percent of the world's total available energy.
While we complained about a trade deficit a year
ago, we made $2 billion in excess of the less
developed countries, depending on our less favored
brethren in Latin America to provide us with one
billion of these dollars in surplus trade balances,
while we provided them with the least aid since aid
began.

How much human peace can you visualize or
expect aboard our spacecraft when its limited resources are so unjustly shared, especially when the
situation is worsening each year? Peace is gained not
by armaments, but by justice. If four-fifths of the
world's people live in misery while the other fifth
enjoy ever greater luxury, then we can expect no

peace aboard Spaceship Earth, only frustration, despair, and ultimately violence. The tragedy is that this is the world that man has made and is making.

Is there any hope for man? Is our spacecraft really hurtling toward massive human disaster: cataclysmic human upheaval and the reduction of this beautiful globe to a burned-out cinder? One can be optimistic, I believe, only if this generation—the young particularly—can shuck off the madness of the nightmare that man for centuries, and increasingly of late, has been living. A new vision is needed if man is to create on earth the beauty that this planet manifests from afar. The vision must be one of social justice, of the interdependence of all mankind. Unless the equality, the oneness, and the common dignity of mankind pervade the vision, the only future of this planet is violence and destruction on an ever increasing scale —a crescendo of inhumanity that can only result in total destruction. As a young man in the Peace Corps in Malawi, Africa, put it, "While our leaders have their power battles and ego trips, countless millions of unknowns are in need of a bit more food, a year or two more of education, another pot or pan, a sensible way of controlling family size, a book or a bicycle. These people aren't asking for much; they would only like to be a bit more free to be a bit more human."

I believe that none but the young—and the young in heart—can dream this vision or pursue this ideal, for it means leaving behind the conventional wisdom that pervades the aging bones of the Western world.

The vision of one peaceful community of mankind on earth, dedicated to justice, equity, and human dignity for all is contrary to most of the modern American myths—unlimited growth for us at the expense of almost everyone else; the absoluteness of our Declaration of Independence; patriotism isolated from every other moral value ("my country right or wrong"); security only by force of arms, however unjustly used (as President Nixon said recently, "Bombs saved lives"); material wealth as the greatest goal of all, since it guarantees pleasure, power, and status. Everything but compassionate, unselfish rectitude.

Who but the young or young in heart can say, I will march to another drumbeat; I will seek another vision for my country and my world? Not a vision of might making right, but of *noblesse oblige*. Not a vision of power, but of honor. Not just honor proclaimed as we hear it proclaimed so loosely today, but honor lived. As Robert Frost said:

> Two roads diverged in a wood, and I—
> I took the one less traveled by,
> And that has made all the difference.

What is mainly needed today to make the difference is a vision of justice to which we, the privileged, commit ourselves anew at home, to demonstrate that if justice is possible here in America, among different races, different religions, different socioeconomic classes, it might just be possible all around the world. America's leadership must be demonstrated at home while it is proclaimed abroad, and that leadership must be inspired by the same kind of vision that inspired the birth of this country: a vision of human equality and dignity needed today for the birth of one whole world, a new planet where human beings aspire to be humane, where beautiful human beings begin to replace the past creations of human ugliness with new creations born of compassion, concern, and competence.

All this is not an empty dream, a naïve vision, if young people, those who will usher in the new millennium, take it seriously, joining intelligence to their idealism, competence to their vision, and the courage to dare to be different in how they view the world they are going to make, or better, remake. I am often asked, "How can we possibly turn the world over to them?" My answer is both simple and obvious: "What other choice do we have? Tomorrow is theirs, not ours."

To pursue the matter further, it would seem to me that we have here one of the strongest calls for continuing education: first, to keep the emerging generation from losing its dreams and goals, and second, even more importantly, to influence the older generation to react better than most of them are reacting at present.

In a world changing as rapidly and profoundly as ours, the older generation, even more than the younger, needs continual reeducation to understand what is happening, what the changes mean, what good and what evil they might portend. The younger generation is by nature supple, changeable, even at times mercurial. The young sway with change, absorb it almost by osmosis, and need but a few changeless points of reference—in principle, in virtue, and in faith—to live with change and still move forward with meaning and direction to their lives. The problem of the older generation is quite the opposite. They face the temptation of the comfortable status quo, the inertia that resists adapting continually to new situations, no matter how promising or exciting. Somehow, continuing education for this older generation must have the same kind of exponential growth in the years ahead as college education has had for the youth in the years just past, if the two generations are to be able to live together in fruitful tension rather than in senseless confrontation.

The very nature of the crisis and the opportunity that face us today would argue for the new assumption that, just as most young people will experience higher education of some kind or other, so education for them and for all who have completed formal higher education will be a continuing process. Just how this process will take place is a matter for further thought, but there is little room for discussion of the necessity of continuing education to undergird positive and constructive social responsibility on the part of the older and younger generations in our society.

Social responsibility must have positive avenues of expression that can be shared equally, if differently, by the young and old members of the society. This positive cooperation is hardly likely to happen unless the young and the old share some reasonably common convictions about the just and reasonable goals of modern society. Some communality of continuing educational experience might well be at the heart of this growing sense of social responsibility, particularly if it is the kind of education in values we spoke of earlier—values taught with the measure of hopefulness and energy that characterizes the best of both generations today.

If one desires a practical expression of this vision we might all begin by a Declaration of the Interdependence of mankind. The evidence is totally on the side of such a declaration—even as regards this country which was founded almost two centuries ago by a Declaration of Independence. There is no serious problem facing our country, and indeed any country today, that is not global in its sweep, as well as in its solution. You can make a whole list: pollution, population, trade, peace, human rights, human development, security, health, education, communication, drugs, crime, energy, space, raw materials, food, freedom, and so forth. Try solving any one of these problems in an adequate way without involving the whole world. Try even thinking about the philosophical implications of an adequate solution without reference to the inherent unity, equality, fraternity, and dignity of mankind and what that dignity demands and requires of human persons everywhere, and most especially those who live where the power, the wealth, and the leverage lie.

I was brought up in an America visualized as

completely separated from the rest of the world, proud of its independence and ocean-insured isolation. Now we learn that the energy that makes all America run—lighted, heated, mechanized, and moved—will depend mainly on sources outside of the United States in another dozen years, and that the fourteen basic metal resources we need for our manufacturing and industrial processes will come mainly from other, less developed countries by the turn of the century. The present energy crisis is just a preview of things to come. The almighty dollar my contemporaries idolized has been devalued twice in less than two years.

Containing communism has been for almost three decades the one all-embracing reason for our doing almost anything abroad, from creating the Marshall Plan to save postwar Europe to destroying Vietnam in order to save it. What validity does containing communism have now when our greatest diplomatic concerns are better relations with the two root sources of communism worldwide, Russia and China? If we can recognize self-interested interdependence in this new relationship with China and Russia, as indeed we must, then we can recognize it anywhere and everywhere. As our students love to sing during liturgical celebrations at Notre Dame, "There's a new world coming, every day, every day." Indeed there is.

It would appear quite obvious at this point that the winds of unity are blowing, that many are working to bridge the chasms that have separated mankind aboard Spaceship Earth. Diplomacy is happily bridging the chasms of ideology. We no longer require that all mankind visualize society exactly as we do. Ecumenism is bringing the Christian and non-Christian religions together in understanding at last. Cultural exchange is finding mutual values in the East and the West, while mercantilism in the modern dress of the multinational corporation is pioneering some unusual ways of economic development between the northern and southern parts of our spacecraft. The energy crisis is pushing for a solution to the Middle Eastern dilemma. Racial prejudice stands convicted worldwide of idiocy when Africans in Uganda expel Orientals who were born there, or when the citizens of Bangladesh cannot forgive their fellow Bihari. Male chauvinism is on the way out in the Western world, belatedly since in the East and Middle East, India and Israel already have female prime ministers. The unity of mankind must be the wave of the future.

This leaves the one great remaining divider of humankind, perhaps the worst of all, national sovereignty. Suppose that an intelligent and cultured visitor from another solar system were to be informed, on seeing our planet as the astronauts saw it from the moon, that in addition to all the inequities, injustices, and alienations already mentioned, mankind on earth insists on governing its spaceship by dividing it into 140 different nationalities, some very large, some impossibly small, and quite a few in between. Our interplanetary visitor would also learn that there is no reasonable rationale for these na-

tional divisions, that they often represent people of
the same language, religion, race, and culture, and
are in fact often separated only by historical accidents. Now that the political separation is a fact, they
are ready to fight to the death to maintain their
national identities and territorial prerogatives. This
visitor could well take off in another direction,
believing that "intelligent life" did not exist here.

Since this is a factual description of how things are
on Spaceship Earth, how difficult it will be to achieve
human unity, decency, and oneness of purpose on
board. We must find some new way of transcending
this inane block of nationality that pits human
against human because by accidents of birth they
happen to be American or Canadian, East or West
German, Venezuelan or Colombian, Kenyan or
Ugandan, North or South Vietnamese.

I would like to propose a solution that would
bypass, rather than cut the Gordian knot of nationality. It is likewise a solution bound to be misunder-
stood unless someone stands in spirit on the moon
and views the world from there, with all its promise
of beauty and unity. As MacLeish said, "To see the
earth as it truly is, small and blue and beautiful in
that eternal silence where it floats, is to see ourselves
as riders on the earth together, brothers on that
bright loveliness in the eternal cold—brothers who
know now they are truly brothers."

What I suggest is that everyone in the world be
allowed to hold dual citizenship—to be a citizen of
the nation in which he or she happens to be born and,

in addition, to be able to qualify for world citizenship. The application to be a citizen of the world, of Spaceship Earth, would involve certain commitments. First, one would have to certify one's belief in the unity of mankind, in the equal dignity of every human being, whatever his or her nationality, race, religion, sex, or color. Second, one would have to certify one's willingness to work for world peace through the promotion and practice of justice at home and abroad. Third, one would have to do something to prove the sincerity of these beliefs, something to promote justice for all, something to promote the peace and well-being of one's fellow humans at home and abroad.

The growing number of human beings on Spaceship Earth who would freely opt for world in addition to national citizenship might begin to prove that men and women are ready to regard each other truly as brothers and sisters, to seek justice for all, to live in peace, to commit their idealism to practice, to transcend nationalistic chauvinism, and to seek to realize a new vision of a Spaceship Earth with liberty and justice for all—the only true road to world peace.

One hopes that whatever international agency would certify this additional world citizenship might also grant to its world citizens some benefits befitting their commitment, such as free passage without visas anywhere in the world—a small concession, but one symbolic of what one free world might be for all its citizens as more of them apply for world passports.*

* Two organizations have pioneered the idea of world citizenship: the World Association of World Federalists (63 Sparks Street, Ottawa,

And one hopes that our country, with its rich transnational, multiracial, and polyreligious population base, might be the first to propose and allow this new idea of dual citizenship for all who desire to give leadership and meaning to this new concept of a more beautiful, more humane Spaceship Earth.

I would like to say for myself, and I hope for many others, that I would welcome this kind of opportunity to declare myself interested in the welfare of mankind everywhere in the world, concerned for the justice due all who suffer injustice anywhere in the world. I believe that being a citizen of the world would enlarge me as a person, would declare my fraternity with every other man, woman, and child in the world. I would take world citizenship to be a firm commitment to work toward a new future for Spaceship Earth and all its passengers, to be a harbinger of hope for all who are close to despair because of their dismal human condition, and finally to be a beacon of light for humanity beleaguered by darkness in so many parts of our world today. Again, one of Notre Dame's Peace Corps volunteers, now studying at Harvard, put it well: "One comes away from an experience like the Peace Corps with a sense of real international brotherhood. The fact that a fellow who had never been out of the Midwest and could speak only English could then live in two countries on the

Canada, K1P 5A6), and the International Registry of World Citizens (California Center, 2959 23rd Avenue, San Francisco, California 94132). I look forward to the time when world citizenship becomes more than a symbolic gesture.

south and eastern fringes of Asia, form deep and lasting friendships with the native people, learn a language and a culture in both Ceylon and Korea and function well in them—it makes one feel a sense of oneness with people all over the world."

I do not see the possibility of world citizenship as a panacea or an immediate answer to all the world's ills and evils. Rather, it would be for each of us a chance to declare our interdependence with one another, our common humanity, our shared hopes, our brotherhood as members of the crew, our common vision of the task facing humanity—to achieve human dignity and the good life together. Once more, Barbara Ward has elucidated the new vision beautifully:

One of the fundamental moral insights of the Western culture which has now swept over the whole globe is that, against all historical evidence, mankind is not a group of warring tribes, but a single, equal and fraternal community. Hitherto, distances have held men apart. Scarcity has driven them to competition and enmity. It has required great vision, great holiness, great wisdom to keep alive and vivid the sense of the unity of man. It is precisely the saints, the poets, the philosophers, and the great men of science who have borne witness to the underlying unity which daily life has denied. But now the distances are abolished. It is at least possible that our new technological resources, properly deployed, will conquer ancient shortage. Can we not at such a time realize the moral unity of our human experience and make it the basis of a patriotism for the world itself?" *

It is easy to scoff at this vision of our humanity, our oneness, our common task as fellow passengers on a small planet. The great and powerful of this earth, including those of America and Europe, can easily sniff cynically and return to their game of power politics, national jealousies, mountains of armaments, millions of graves of men mourned by widows and orphans, ravaged oceans, unverdant plains, and hungry homeless people who despair of the good life. But somehow I believe there is enough good will in our country and in the world to expect millions of people to declare all of this powerful posturing of corrupt politicians to be arrant nonsense in one world, to say that we do want all men and women to be brothers and sisters, that we do believe in justice and peace, and that we think homes, fields of grain, schools, and medicine are better than guns, tanks, submarines, ABMs and MIRVs. The trouble is that the millions of little people, the ones who really man Spaceship Earth, the ones who really work and suffer and die while the politicians posture and play, these little ones have never been given a chance to declare themselves. And this is wrong, globally wrong.

Having traveled across the face of our beautiful planet, having traversed all its oceans and its continents, having shared deep human hopes with my

* *Spaceship Earth*, p. 148.

brothers and sisters of every nationality, religion, color, and race, having broken bread and found loving friendship and brotherhood everywhere on earth, I am prepared this day to declare myself a citizen of the world, and to invite everyone everywhere to embrace this vision of our interdependent world, our common humanity, our noblest hopes and our common quest for justice in our times and, ultimately, for peace on earth, now, and in the next millennium.